MILITARY AIR TRANSPORT

AIRLIFT

THE ILLUSTRATED HISTORY

MILITARY AIR TRANSPORT

AIRLIFT

THE ILLUSTRATED HISTORY

RICHARD TOWNSHEND BICKERS

OSPREY
AEROSPACE

Published in Great Britain in 1998
Osprey Publishing Limited,
Michelin House, 81 Fulham Road, London SW3 6RB

ISBN 1 85532 693 0

Originated and produced by PW Publishing Limited
Broadstone, England

Editor: Jasper Spencer-Smith

Page make-up by Goodall James, Bournemouth, England

Reprographics by SDR Limited, Broadstone, England

Set in 10pt on 11.5pt Bembo

ACKNOWLEDGEMENTS

I wish to thank the Royal Aeronautical Society, the Royal Air Force Museum, the Imperial War Museum, the Airborne Forces Museum and the Public Record Office for their invaluable and friendly help with my research for this book. Also my thanks to Hugh Cowin *(HC)*, Philip Jarrett *(PJ)*, Jay Miller *(JM)*, Bruce Robertson *(BR)* and Bill Hunt at the Ministry of Defence *(MOD)* photographic archive for supplying the superb illustrations for the book.

Richard Townshend Bickers
Shoscombe, April 1998

Title pages: Blackburn Beverlys of No 47 Squadron, Royal Air Force. (BR)

Northrop C-125A Raider takes off with rocket (JATO) assistance. *(HC)*

CONTENTS

CHAPTER ONE

Supplies by Air

The need for transport aircraft is as great as the more obvious one for bombers and fighters, but it was given little attention before, during and after the First World War until the 1930s.

The great venture and adventure of carrying troops and war materiel by air is no less enthralling than the long history of battle. Logistics – the moving, quartering and supply of an army, air force or navy – is as important a factor of strategy as tactics, reconnaissance, intelligence, victualling, medical services, the fighting quality of the opposing forces and the capability of their weapons. The air movement of supplies and personnel is also as hazardous in its own way as going into action. It must confront the vagaries of weather and the nature of the terrain from which transport aircraft have to take off, over which they must fly and on which they will land. On campaign they operate mostly from temporary airfields where the ground is rough and there is scant space for safe take-off and landing. The crews have no active means of defence and are frequently at risk of attack by fighter and ground fire. The threat of engine or airframe defects, failures of oxygen supply or forced landings is always present.

The need for transport aircraft is as great as the more obvious one for bombers and fighters, but it was given little attention before, during and after the First World War until the 1930s. Strategically, the movement of armies in the Second World War had to be done by sea, but the supply of reinforcements and military stores from rations to ammunition and vehicles began to be done by air. Tactically, aircraft became essential in reacting quickly to an enemy threat, delivering essential supplies to a beleaguered garrison and evacuating casualties. Powered aeroplanes and gliders needed to be robust, mechanically reliable and have ample carrying capacity, which, in the early days of the Second World War, they lacked. There was one paramount condition that was the decisive factor in planning such missions: the side that is carrying it out must have air superiority. Transport aircraft were slow and towing a glider made them even slower, easy targets for fighter attack and anti-aircraft guns.

It became routine for transport squadrons to go where, as Douglas Bader put it in the context of all types of operation, "the hot lead was flying": carrying supplies as well as paratroops and others of all arms to the battlefield, not to a rear area.

In 1909 the first international air show, a week long, was held at Rheims: *La Grande Semaine d'Aviation*. Hitherto no government had committed itself to spending money on aeroplanes. This show was proof of their potential usefulness. In 1910 France, Germany and Russia formed air forces and Britain followed suit the next year. The only perceived functions of an aeroplane were reconnaissance and artillery spotting. Some armies had used tethered balloons for these purposes. The possibility of aeroplanes carrying troops or military supplies was slow to find expression.

In its early days air transport was a matter of improvisation. There is a widespread erroneous belief that the first aeroplane ever built which could, if manufactured in sufficient numbers, have been adapted to carry military reinforcements, supplies and casualties was the Grahame – White

"Charabanc". Why else would he have called it by the French for omnibus, *char-à-banc*? It was actually called the Aerobus. And it was not until 2 October 1913 that he took it up on a demonstration flight with nine passengers – a payload of 1,372lb (622kg) – and was airborne for 20 minutes before landing safely. This is usually claimed to be a world record. It was not.

The facts are that a Frenchman whose name stands high in the annals of early aeronautics and aeronauts, Louis Breguet, took 11 passengers up on 23 March 1911 in an aeroplane of his own design. On the following day, another French designer, Roger Sommer, flew with 12 passengers aboard in one of his machines.

Any of those three aeroplanes could have been prototypes of military transport aircraft if anybody had thought that these new-fangled flying machines showed promise of being useful in carrying soldiers. Interest, however, was more in races and distance records than war.

The record number of passengers set by Sommer was surpassed by the first four-engine aircraft. Built in Russia at the Baltic Railway Car factory, it was designed by Igor Sikorsky, whose inventive genius did not extend to nomenclature, for he gave it the banal name *Bolshoi*, which means big. This has not prevented British aviation writers from imitating their French counterparts and consistently calling it "Le Grand". True, the Russian aristocracy affected to speak French rather than their native language, but that is not a plausible reason for the misnomer.

On 11 February 1914 its pilot flew this massive aeroplane with 16 passengers aboard.

For the next 10 years, in Britain and other countries makeshift modifications had to be made to bomber aeroplanes for the accommodation of passengers. The environments in which the countries competing to advance the development of aviation were working was typical of their national characters.

In Germany, airships still had precedence over aeroplanes. In Russia, size was the main criterion. In America, the Wright brothers had given a useful lead. Logic suggested that either the USA, as the inventor of the first flying machines, Germany, with its desire for territorial expansion and prominence in building airships, or Russia, whose engineers thought in terms commensurate with its vast size, would produce the first military aircraft big enough to carry troops in great numbers. This, of course, happened when *Bolshoi* took to the air and was soon followed by Sikorsky's *Ilya Mourometz* bomber that operated in the First World War. Although the war accelerated the development of more powerful and efficient aero engines and the design and construction of bigger and faster aircraft, it was not until its last year that aeroplanes with a 100ft (30m) wingspan emerged from the British factories in large numbers.

As soon as peace was declared, with its dazzling commercial prospects for the aviation industry, the leading industrial nations began to forge ahead in every aspect of aviation. The emphasis put on

Above: **A German Zeppelin with its floating shed at Friedrichshafen on Lake Constance. Zeppelins of similar type were used in November 1917 to supply, without success, Tanganyika a German colony then called German East Africa.**
(BR)

Above: **The first ever food relief flight took place in 1916 was by RFC and RNAS aircraft at Kut-el-Amara in Mesoptamia (Iraq).** *(BR)*

airliners that would carry an increasing number of passengers was beneficial to the design of bigger bombers, military freight carriers and air ambulances. Until the Second World War, some military aircraft had a double function as bomber/personnel or bomber/freight carriers. It was only as this war progressed that purpose-designed troop carriers, freighters and ambulances began to proliferate and became an essential, though unarmed, adjunct to the

types that dropped bombs, launched torpedoes or rockets and fired guns.

It was not only the equipment available that held back progress towards air-minded armies; it was more the rigidity of the military attitude. General Staffs were slow to perceive the advantages that would accrue from combined operations by air and ground forces. The few senior officers who did take an interest in combined operations either achieved little or became subject to jealousy and the intrigue between the armed services that is an unsavoury facet of military life. The Italian General Giulio Douhet, who was much respected in the world of military aviation, formed the world's first combined army and air force unit in which ground troops trained to use parachutes were flown by airmen. It proved to be a waste of time. When Russia trained military parachutists, however, nobody dared to be obstructive and thereby face a firing squad. The USSR soon had the world's only efficient paratroop formation. In Germany, when General Kurt Student was ordered to form a paratroop regiment, he was hindered by his equals.

When the first British parachute unit was formed, Germany was taken as a pattern: the essential requirement was perceived to be the use of huge

numbers for airborne and parachute attacks. Since the Second World War it has become clear that the means of transporting the troops is just as important as numbers. The obvious necessity to design and build fighters and bombers of constantly improved performance is now matched by an equal acknowledgement of the need to give the same attention to transport aircraft, both fixed- and rotary-wing.

How it Began

It is generally accepted that the French were the first to use air transportation for military purposes, because they operated a balloon service to communicate with the rest of the country when Paris was under siege during the war with Prussia in 1870–71. Frenchmen were the keenest of the early balloonists and the Montgolfier brothers, Joseph and Etienne, had made the first balloon to carry passengers. Its maiden ascent was on 21 November 1783.

The first military use of tethered observation balloons was made by the Army of the North in America's Civil War, when, on its outbreak in 1861, President Lincoln ordered the creation of a balloonist corps comprising 10 balloons and 100 men. Messages between air and ground were exchanged by wire telegraph, and photographs were taken from aloft. Aerial photography had been invented in 1859 by a French designer, caricaturist,

Above: **A BE 2c of No 14 Squadron RFC in Palestine where they were deployed on Army co-operation duties. The BE2 entered RFC service in February 1913 and was used in various roles throughout World War One. It was powered by a 70 hp Renault V8 water-cooled engine.** *(BR)*

Left: **The Handley Page HP.11, 0/400 was designed originally as a heavy night bomber but was later used in World War One as a transport. After the Armistice many 0/400's were converted to civilian airliners for that growing industry.** *(MOD)*

photographer and devotee of flight, Felix Tournachon, who used the pseudonym Nadar. It was improved by an American named King two years later. Nadar, however, trumped his ace in 1868 by inventing micro-photography.

Prussia provoked France into declaring war on 19 July 1870. It ended on 2 September with the surrender of Napoleon III and his army after the Battle of Sedan. The Prussians then marched on Paris and put the city under siege from 20 September until January 1871. In Metz, which was besieged early in the Prussian invasion, an attempt had been made to communicate by free balloons and several small ones were hastily made and released, unmanned. Some landed in French hands, others in the enemy's. Disappointing though this was, it pointed the way. The last mail train had left Paris on 18 September and the capital was now cut off from all forms of correspondence. Attempts were made to convey letters by road and river, without success. Before this, a group of balloonists–Nadar, Dartois, Durouf, Tissandier and Fonvielle–had offered to use captive observation balloons to report on the enemy's activities. This was accepted under the aegis of a Colonel Usquin and three balloons owned and crewed by Nadar, Eugéne Godard and Wilfrid de Fonvielle were sent up. Sailors on duty in the Paris forts and detachments of the auxiliary engineers in the National Guard were detailed to help in positioning the balloons and to carry reports on the balloonists' observations to General Trochu, in command of the capital's defence.

From 19 September, however, before Tissandier was able to put up a fourth balloon, Paris was completely invested. Communication now took priority over observation, particularly with the government, which had been transferred to Tours. On the declaration of war, Tissandier and Fonvielle had offered to follow the French Army with a captive balloon, but were refused. Over the present issue, which was as much a civilian matter as a military one, the postal authorities and Telegraph Department consulted the balloonists at once about the means of setting up a postal service by air.

The Army did not establish or control the operation, nor were troops carried into battle. Military despatches were included in the mail, but carrying them was not the sole purpose. On only one occasion was the pilot a soldier, Private Lacaze. He was blown out to sea and never found. Thirty sailors who had volunteered to be balloon pilots qualified after only two hours' instruction. When a balloon was ready to leave Paris, the letters were taken to it by Monsieur Brechet, Director of the Post Office Department, and Monsieur Chassinot, Director of the Seine Post Office. No military authority handled the transmission of mail. Before take-off, the latest weather information was given to the pilots by a M. Herv Mangon.

A Frenchman named Dagron had invented a method of micro-photography that reduced the print to one quarter of the size of a playing card and contained 2,000 letters or figures. All correspondence was conducted by this means, which greatly reduced the bulk and weight of the cargo.

On 23 September Jules Duron took off at 0745 hrs in a balloon that belonged to the Post Office, to deliver 276lb (125kg) of mail. Baffled Austrian soldiers saw him flit past overhead unmolested and he landed at 1130hrs near the Château de Cracouville, 3.7 miles (6km) from Evreux.

The next trip was made two days later by Gabriel Mangin in a balloon belonging to the Ministry of Works, at 1100 hrs with 670lb (304kg) of mail, a passenger, Monsieur Lutz, and three carrier pigeons to take messages back to Paris: the prevailing easterly winds foiled any hope of returning there by balloon.

On the 29th, deliveries were made by two balloons in tandem, actually attached to each other. The Post Office owned both. They were flown by yet another famous balloonist, Louis Godard. All balloons bore a name. The one he occupied was called *Napoleon* and its Siamese twin was *Hirondelle*. For this conjoint operation they were whimsically christened "*Etats-Unis*". There was one passenger,

M. Courtins, and six pigeons went with him. The tandem balloons were fired at but landed safely at 1330hrs near Nantes.

It is usually stated that henceforth all flights were made by night. This is not so. The balloon on the fourth trip was airborne at 0930 on 30 September. The first night flight was not made until 18 November by the 31st balloon to set out. The take-off was at 2315hrs and it landed at Luzarches, near Pontoise, at 0800hrs. Altogether only 27 night flights were made.

During the four months and five days of the investment, 66 flights were made, 30 of them by the sailors; 102 passengers travelled, 11 tonnes of mail and about 400 pigeons accompanied them. Of the 363 pigeons released, only 57 made it back to the capital.

The Post Office Department owned 48 of the balloons, the Telegraph Department owned eight, the Ministry of Works and the Ministry of Education each owned one. The rest were privately owned and lent to the Post Office.

The Prussians made a special mobile gun with which to shoot down balloons, but did not hit any. Earlier in the century there had been two proposals for the use of aircraft for transporting troops. Both were for belligerent purposes. The first was put forward by Napoleon's staff in 1805, to invade England. Their ludicrous scheme was to send a big enough force across the English Channel by balloon.

The most obvious reason for rejecting the plan was that air currents would scatter them over a large area, whereas the first necessity of an invasion is to land an entire force in a small area at the same time. This would have been impossible because all the balloons could not take off together. Each could lift only four men, so at least 1,250 balloons would be needed. Once a balloon was filled with hydrogen it had to be released within a few minutes, otherwise even the slightest breeze would blow it sideways and tip it over, make it collide with others or tear the gasbag apart from the basket. Even before reaching that stage there was a more basic obstacle: where could a big enough area of flat ground be found on which to assemble the force? A balloon canopy spread on the ground took up a lot of space until it was filled with gas. Napoleon, of course, dismissed the notion.

The second impractical suggestion was also to invade England. The Wright brothers had made their first flights in 1903 and Blériot flew the Channel in 1909, but already, in 1908, Germany considered the practicality of ordering 50,000

Above: **The RE8 was used throughout World War One as an artillery spotting/ observation aircraft. On 14 July 1918, RE 8's of No 3 Squadron, Australian Flying Corps carried out an air supply drop of ammunition to troops of the 4th Australian Division. The aircraft shown F 6048 was re-built, in France, from salvaged parts.**

Wright B types with which to make a landing on the south coast. Even 5,000 would have taken years to build.

These two fatuous notions were bred by ignorance. An intelligent one was made by Brigadier-General William ("Billy") Mitchell, Commander of the Air Service in the United States First Army in France. In November 1918 he recommended that an infantry division be parachuted into Metz, to take the enemy from the rear. He expected the fighting to continue into 1919, which would give time to train the troops and muster an adequate number of aircraft. The proposal might have been adopted, but the enemy surrendered a few days later, on 11 November.

A true use of air transport to supply an army in the field had been attempted in 1917. Tanganyika, the biggest and richest of Germany's colonies, then called German East Africa, was defended by an army of native troops officered by Germans.

On the east it bordered on a British protectorate, Kenya, and on its western border lay a Belgian colony. General von Lettow-Forbeck, commanding the Tanganyikan force, compensated for the difficulties posed by the terrain and an outnumbering British and Indian Army garrison by using guerrilla tactics brilliantly.

In 1917 an expeditionary force of British, Belgian and South African contingents, commanded by the Afrikaner General Smuts, set off to drive the

Below: **Britain's largest bomber of World War One was the Handley Page V/1500. Powered by four (in push/pull nacelles) 375 hp Rolls-Royce Eagle VIII V-12 water-cooled engines, the V/1500 was the first true strategic bomber in history but was not used in action. After the war the RAF used the aircraft in the transport role, whilst Handley Page re-designed it as a successful airliner.** *(BR)*

855

Germans out. A Zeppelin commanded by Kapitanleutnant Ludwig Bockholt set off from Jamboli, in Bulgaria, on 21 November 1917 to deliver supplies for von Lettow-Vorbeck. Staging through Turkey and Crete, it arrived at Khartoum two days later.

Reading British wireless messages, Bockholt concluded that the defenders had been beaten, so he returned to the Fatherland. In reality, although Lettow-Forbeck withdrew to adjacent Portuguese Africa, he continued to harass his enemies until the Armistice. As this mission was aborted, it can be regarded only as an attempt to supply by air.

Forty-five years were to pass after France's claim in 1870 before the first real military airlift, in the true sense of the word, actually to deliver a cargo, was flown. Britain's Royal Flying Corps (RFC) carried it out. Again, it was an improvisation to cope with a siege, but the circumstances were greatly different and there is no doubt of its entitlement to be described as a military undertaking.

The Great War 1914-18

The country where air drops were initiated was then called Mesopotamia and is now Iraq. Kut-el-Amara straggles along the eastern bank of a mile-wide curve on the Tigris 270 miles (435km) up-river from Basra, Iraq's seaport 35 miles (55km) inland from the Persian (now Arabian) Gulf. In 1916 both towns were maladorous and insanitary. Oil from the many great wells of the region was essential to Britain. Turkey, Germany's ally, coveted the oilfields. Two Indian Army Divisions sent to protect them captured Basra on 21 November 1914.

In August 1915 the Division commanded by Major-General Charles Townshend (later knighted), was ordered to advance on Baghdad. It fought its way to within 20 miles (32km) of the city before being forced to retreat to Kut in December. Here Townshend's force was besieged. Repeated assaults by British and Indian troops much weakened by dysentery and casualties in action failed to penetrate the enemy positions.

No need for reinforcement or supply by air had been foreseen by any country's military planners. Initially, aeroplanes were regarded as useful only for reconnaissance and artillery spotting – telling the gunners how close to the target their shells were falling. Next, they carried bombs. In 1915 some began to be armed with machine guns, to escort and protect unarmed aircraft and to engage the enemy in single combat.

Despite this versatility, the military mind had not entertained the notion that one of the aeroplane

Above: **Used as a two-seater bomber in World War One, the Airco (De Havilland) DH.4, became the mainstay of post-war communication squadrons. A total of 4846, DH 4's were built and most were powered by a Rolls-Royce Eagle VIII engine.** *(PJ)*

manufacturers should be capable of designing one that could carry a big cargo. Presumably, for instance, Britain's War Office was unaware of Grahame-White's or Sikorsky's work.

Some 6,000 Arabs inhabited Kut. The defending garrison numbered 11,600 combatant soldiers and 3,500 non-combatant. Among them were five Royal Flying Corps officers, 40 other ranks and four aircraft – all unserviceable. Townshend had had a hospital built to accommodate 600 patients, but there were soon thousands of sick and wounded. Still, nobody thought of supplying the beleaguered force with medical supplies, food and ammunition by air. If any bright staff officer had mooted air drops, no action would have been feasible: the 6th Division, fighting to raise the seige, possessed 14 assorted RFC and Royal Naval Air Service (RNAS) types, few of which were serviceable at any one time.

In October 1916 the existing gallimaufry of aeroplanes became A Flight of No 30 Squadron. B Flight had two BE2Cs. In December C Flight was formed, comprising one Maurice Farman and one BE2C: for the next two months these last two were the only aircraft serviceable in the Mesopotamian Theatre. However, by 11 April 1916 30 Sqdn's strength in BE2Cs was up to eight.

Sickness was rife in Kut and the river had flooded the area. Townshend signalled General Headquarters in Basra to report that all food except horseflesh would be consumed by 29 April. At an HQ conference someone made an inspired suggestion of the obvious: if aeroplanes could drop bombs, they must surely be able to drop cargo. The Aviation Officer calculated that the minimum requirement was 5,000lb (2,270kg), which would give each man a hardly Lucullan portion of six ounces (170g). This could be dropped if 70 per cent of the aircraft on strength flew three daily sorties. The General Officer Commanding, Lieutenant-General Sir Percy Lake, accordingly ordered a maximum effort; subject to urgent requests for artillery observation and reconnaissance.

On 13 January 1916 spare parts for guns, wireless sets and the Division's river launch, medical supplies and newspapers had been free-dropped. Four days later a 70lb millstone was parachuted.

For the planned air supply four BE2Cs of 30 Sqdn plus three Short floatplanes, one Henry Farman and one Voisin of the RNAS were detailed. Adequate packing and a reliable method of dropping had to be devised. To allow maximum payload, BE2C pilots would fly without an observer. Captain Eric Murray, commanding B Flight, goes down in history as the first to invent a way of adapting a bomb rack to carry freight. A bar was fitted to it, pivoted at one end and locked at the other by a quick-release device operated by the pilot. Two sacks were sewn together at the top and slung across the bar. When one end of the bar was released it dropped and the load slid off. Two sacks were used, one inside the other: if the inner sack tore, the outer one retained the contents.

At the first trial, with a 200lb (90kg) burthen, the BE2C tipped on to its nose while taxying for take-off. Thereafter the sacks were more evenly disposed about the centre of gravity. The best arrangement proved to be two 25lb (11kg) sacks on the bar and two 50lb (23kg) tied on each of the lower mainplanes. These latter were fastened by a slipknot that the pilot loosened or cut, then pulled each sack over the trailing edge. Wind resistance reduced speed almost to the stall. Experienced pilots were allowed to fly with a 200lb (90gk) load. The same way of loading was possible on the Voisin (150lb/68kg) and Farman (200lb/90kg), but the Short floatplane had to carry two packs of 200–250lb (90–113kg) under the bomb rack, held by a broad canvas band and released by the pilot.

The first 20 sorties were flown on 14 April and 3500lb (1,588kg) dropped. The dropping zone was on the outskirts of Kut. One sack fell in the river and one behind enemy lines.

Throughout the period of these operations 10 per cent of the loads were lost in this manner because the sacks did not all have the same shape or, therefore, trajectory. Pilots had to fly between 5,000ft (1,525m) and 7,000ft (2,135m) to avoid anti-aircraft and heavy small-arms fire. Accuracy of aim deteriorated with height; also, the longer the drop, the greater the effect of wind and of an individual sack's aerodynamics.

Aircraft serviceability and the weather made it impossible to fly daily or make the same number of sorties per day when the missions were flown. Pilot strength, also, was affected by dysentery, diarrhoea and other ailments. Added to these factors was the intrusion by hostile aircraft. On the second day 1,333lb (605kg) fell within the target area while a large share went to the Turks. On the 17, 18 and 19 April only three, five and two sorties respectively were possible.

On 23 April a mere one sortie was made but a total of 32 were flown during the next three days. On the 24th a Fokker shadowed two BE2Cs and on the 26th three of them shot down a Short Seaplane, killing the observer and wounding the pilot. Another BE2C was attacked and its pilot wounded. On 29 April Kut surrendered.

In the British Army, all ranks from private to Field Marshal were ignorant of aviation and its problems with aircraft serviceability, air crew illness and enemy air attack. Consequently the expressed opinion of the ground-grippers was that the attempt at air supply had failed through the RFC's fault.

It was not until 4 July 1918 that ground troops again received air drops. This time it was on the Western Front and No 3 Squadron of the Australian Flying Corps carried out the operation, the last of its kind in that war. The BE2C had been a fragile

little aeroplane with a 90hp engine and best speed of 72mph (116km/h). The RE8 that the Australians were flying was a beefy sort with a 140hp motor and top speed of 92mph (148km/h). The requirement was to supply the 4th Australian Division with small arms ammunition. This was done by fitting metal cans to the bomb racks, each containing a parachute of aircraft fabric 14ft (4. 3m) in diameter with a small hole in the middle. Attached under each can and to the parachute were two boxes, holding 2,000 rounds of . 303 ammunition apiece. Flying at 800ft (245m), the observer released them by a bowden cable and their weight dragged the 'chutes out of the cans. From mid-morning until 1500hrs 12 "Harry Tates" – named after a leading music hall comedian – each averaged 30-minute sorties and dropped 93 boxes on six aiming points. August saw more supplies delivered by air. No 32 Sqdn's Armstrong Whitworth FK 8s with a 160hp Beardmore engine, which had just come into service, dropped thousands of rounds of ammunition as the enemy was being driven back in the Battle of Bapaume. Next day No 53's RE8s delivered more as well as barbed wire and flares. No 82 Sqdn's FK8s and No 7's RE8s dropped a total of 63 boxes of ammunition in 32 sorties.

In September Allied forces in the Middle East called for help again. This time it was from the Syrian Desert, where the column advancing on Damascus was being strafed and bombed by four German aeroplanes. The Royal Air Force (on 1 April 1918 the two British flying Services had been combined under this name) positioned two Bristol Fighters at Umm-es-Surab, a landing ground in "the blue". The Brisfit was the world's sturdiest fighter,

armed with a Vickers machine gun firing forward and a Lewis covering flanks and rear. The 275hp Rolls-Royce engine gave it 113mph (182km/h). It had done great execution on the Western Front and was now going to do the same in an area that the enemy thought would be out of British reach.

There indeed was a problem: how to provide the aircraft with ammunition and all the means of maintenance. The solution was the world's biggest bomber, a Handley Page 0/400 with its 100ft (30m) wingspan, two Rolls-Royce 322hp engines, speed of 97mph (156km/h), eight hours endurance and 765 miles (1,230km) range. One of these monsters arrived with a ton of petrol, oil and spares.

During the following month two supply drops were delivered on the Western Front. On the 2nd and 3rd, the Belgians and French were held up in the Houthulst Forest. Nos 82 and 218 Sqdns FK8s and DH9s delivered rations for them in sandbags partly filled with earth to cushion the impact. The final delivery by air was made on 13 October 1918. The town of Le Cateau was still being defended by enemy machine-ßgun nests after the rest of the garrison had been driven out. The inhabitants were starving. The FK8s of No 35 Sqdn brought them two tons of bully beef and biscuits.

The immediate future for military transportation by air was far from predictable, despite the capabilities it had demonstrated. In Britain the junior Service was an object of great jealousy from the other two. Although these quarrelled with each other, they were united in insisting that now the Great War was over there would be no need for an independent air force.

Above: **The BE2 was designed by Geoffrey de Havilland and F.M. Green and built at the Royal Aircraft Factory, first flying in 1911. The aircraft shown A3074 was built by Wolseley Motors, one of around 22 firms constructing them. It served with No 26 Squadron RAF in East Africa.** *(BR)*

CHAPTER TWO

Communication Flights

In the early months of peacetime there were no commercial airlines. The air forces that had fought the war owned the best aircraft, pilots and crews.

The Armistice on 11 November 1918 meant that fewer demands would be made of the Army and Navy, but it brought no rest for the Royal Air Force. This was welcomed by the junior Service.

Flying is a cult. Most cavalry officers choose their arm, even though it is mechanised, because they are keen horsemen and equestrian sport is still their favourite pastime, with its own jargon and attributes. Some men choose the Navy from a love of life at sea, which also has its own dialect and sorcery. Airmen volunteer to fly because there is a mystique among pilots, both military and civilian, which creates a stronger bond than those others and an international fraternity that no outsider can fully understand. In both world wars the opposing air forces have shown courtesy and even chivalry towards opponents they have shot down. This is not customary in those who have been enemies on land or at sea. Airmen's attitude to the other arms has always been one of mildly amused tolerance of the old fashioned.

Pilots share a special fellowship in having mastered a difficult expertise and being privy to an esoteric language. They share with their crews a sheer delight in the freedom of the sky, the beauty of cloud formations and of lands and seascapes seen from a vantage that no landsman or sailor knows. Who but an airman can see the sun rise more than once on the same day by a change of altitude? The war was over, but thousands of soldiers and airmen remained in France on duty. Senior officers of all the armed forces, politicians and diplomats attended conferences in Paris. Widespread communications had to be maintained. The RAF provided the means.

At the request of the Foreign Office, the Air Ministry began two daily messenger flights by DH4s on 14 December 1914 between London and Paris for the Peace Delegation that met at Versailles. For passengers, a Handley Page 0/400 was also provided.

This was the start of a service that soon had to satisfy greater demands. On 27 July 1919 No 1 (Communications) Squadron was formed for long-distance trips, which had to be authorised by the Chief of the Air Staff. A Flight was equipped with the DH4, a two-seater bomber with nearly four hours' endurance and 136mph (219km/h) top speed. B Flight's aircraft, which were only for Air Ministry officers, comprised two Avro 504s and two BE2Es. Both types were two-seater elementary trainers. The former had entered squadron service in 1918 and could attain 85mph (137km/h); the latter had appeared in the last few weeks of the war and was 3mph (4.8km/h) slower. Crossing the Channel was not always what the RAF calls "a piece of cake": on foggy days it had to be flown at a height of 10 to 12ft (3 to 3.6m).

During the war, flights had been over short distances. Of the first four squadrons to fly to France, two were stationed in Wiltshire and one in Hampshire: all had to refuel at Dover. The fourth, in Scotland, took nine days to get there. For the next four years squadrons were based close behind their own front line, hence most sorties were over familiar

territory and landmarks. The exceptions were strategic bombing operations against targets in France and Germany that began in October 1917. It was not until June 1918 that bombers began to make raids by night. Few pilots were experienced in long cross-country or night flying and aircraft seldom had wireless sets, operated by the observer or air gunner, to keep in touch with the ground by Morse code. Every facet of communication was developing fast and in June Nos 57 and 110 Squadrons fitted radio-telephones with 20 miles (32km) range.

The communications squadron was unable to cope with all the work that it was asked to do. On 13 December No 86 (Communications) Wing was established with two squadrons. Each had an HP 0/400, converted to accommodate eight passengers, and four DH 8's with two passengers in a compartment made by enlarging the rear cockpit. No 1 Sqdn remained at Hendon; No 2 was based at Versailles. DH10s of 120 Squadron, stationed at Hawkinge, carried mail to and from Cologne for the British Army On The Rhine. The risks inherent in what was still a pioneering era, with engines and airframes that were not totally reliable, no efficient long-range radio communication and in bad weather that was not accurately predictable, were heightened by the RAF's refusal to issue parachutes. In October 1919 they were allowed for Avro 504K trainers, but were not provided for other types until 1921 and did not come into general service until 1925.

Major-General Sir Frederick Sykes, Chief of the Air Staff, described the hazards of low-level crossings over the English Channel with the crew's and passengers' goggles smeared with oil, sleet or both. On one occasion he and his pilot were faced unexpectedly with the Sussex cliffs and a steep climb to clear them. Another time, seeking Croydon, his aircraft nearly collided with the dome of St Paul's Cathedral, so his pilot diverted to Northolt. Pilots could have been excused if they regarded flying Sykes with trepidation: he was no lucky mascot. Captain E. M. Knott had barely set off with him in a DH4 for Paris when, at 200ft (60m), the engine seized, the aircraft stalled into the ground and the pilot was killed. A mechanic had neglected to fill the radiator. Sykes's next misadventure occurred when he became Controller General of Civil Aviation. Aircraft were grounded by bad weather, but Lieutenant E. Drew risked flying him from Paris to Hendon. They took off in a snowstorm, clambered to 10,000ft (3,050m), two hours later were in sunshine and descended through cloud to verify Drew's navigation. The engine suddenly failed, they crashed and found that they were 70 miles (113km) off course.

These communication flights in all weathers yielded valuable diverse information. For instance, it was found that many hours' flying in rain and hail could wear an inch (25mm) off the leading edge of a propeller blade. The problem was cured by fitting metal tips.

By August 1919 a large part of the British Occupation Force on the Continent had been

Above: **A Bristol F2B flies low over the desert floor to collect a message suspended on a wire between two poles. The F2 was first delivered to RFC in December 1916 with the final example delivered to the RAF in December 1926. The aircraft was mainly powered by a 275 hp Rolls-Royce Falcon III V-12 water-cooled engine; up to 16 different engine types, ranging from 120 to 400 hp, were also fitted.** *(PJ)*

Right: **After World War One many Airco DH.4 bombers were converted to communications and staff transport aircraft. This example, F5764, was converted by Palladium Autocars in 1919 and has a newly constructed aft-fuselage cabin, for two passengers, over what was the air-gunner's position.** *(BR)*

Below: **Originally conceived as twin-engined, three-seat day bomber the De Havilland DH.10 Amiens was used on pioneering flights for postal and communications services.** *(BR)*

repatriated. The communications squadrons ceased carrying mail and the Post Office took over.

The First Empire Air Routes

In the early months of peacetime there were no commercial airlines. The air forces that had fought the war owned the best aircraft, pilots and crews. The RAF was the first to make intercontinental flights, which it began even before the war was over. For gaining experience of long–distance flying it enjoyed the advantage of serving the world's most widespread empire, with squadrons based in the Middle East and India.

These pioneering flights began on 28 July 1918, when a Handley Page 0/400 flown by Major A. S. C. Maclaren took off from England for Egypt, where he landed on 7 August. Two months later he again flew an 0/400 from England to Egypt and was

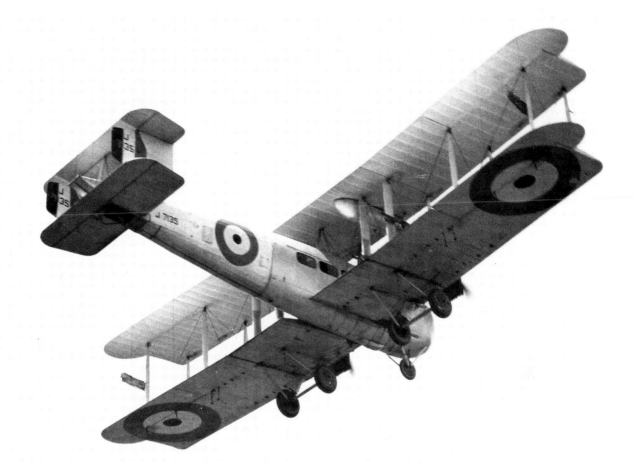

rewarded with the Air Force Cross. On 29 November Captain Ross Smith flew an 0/400 from Cairo to Baghdad with a night stop at Damascus. Maclaren's next long flight was to India. His second pilot, Captain Robert Halley, DFC and bar, formerly of the Royal Naval Air Service, was one of the RAF's best flyers. When the RFC and RNAS were combined, the Independent Air Force, stationed in eastern France, had been formed to bomb the most important targets in France, Belgium and Germany. Some of its squadrons flew DH4s by day; others, Halley's among them, Handley Page 0/100s and 0/400s at night. It was on these that he had won his decorations. With him and Maclaren on the flight to India were two fitters, Sergeants A. E. Smith and W. Crockett, and a rigger, Sgt T. Brown. Also aboard, on his way to take over as Air Officer Commanding India, was Brigadier-General N. D. K. McEwen, MC. Their aircraft, an HP V1500, was the war's biggest British type but had never flown in anger. It was on stand-by at Bircham Newton, Norfolk, to bomb Berlin, when peace was declared. Its four Rolls-Royce 375hp Eagle engines were back-to-back in pairs; it was 64ft (19.5m) long, with a 126ft (38.4m) wingspan. Two extra 75 gallon (341 litre) petrol tanks had been installed. It was so unstable that it could not be trimmed to fly straight and level, so had to be flown hands-on all the way.

The pilots made a droll contrast. Maclaren stood over six feet (183cm), Halley was nine inches (23cm) shorter and had twice failed air crew selection for this reason. When eventually accepted, he had, like many of the shortest – and best – pilots in both world wars, to sit on a cushion. Maclaren and McEwen had both been at Charterhouse School, so it was typical of the era that they named their machine "Old Carthusian", which was painted on its bows and must have puzzled the British Other Ranks, let alone the people of many nationalities who saw it on its journey.

Bad weather postponed the scheduled departure from 28 November 1918 to 7 December 1918. After this ill-natured aeroplane – its prototype had crashed four weeks after its first flight – did take off from Martlesham Heath, in Suffolk, it had to return to base with engine trouble. It finally got away on 13 January 1919, ran into thick cloud and, having no wireless, landed at Bergues, near Dunkirk. Two days later it continued to le Bourget, on the outskirts of Paris.

On 15 January Maclaren took off for Rome, but the weather forced landings at Beaune and Pisa. Crew and passengers had hoped to fly direct from Rome to Athens but the *Old Carthusian* could not make enough height to cross the Alps; so they followed the Italian coast to Catania, in Sicily. The

Above: **As a development of the Vickers Vimy bomber, the Vickers Vernon was designed specifically as a troop carrier. Originally powered by two Rolls-Royce Eagle VIII engines it was found to be underpowered in desert conditions and was re-engined with 450 hp Napier Lion engines. The Vernon carried a crew of two and 12 passengers.** *(PJ)*

deeply muddy airfield nearly caused the aircraft to pitch onto its nose. Italian troops spent many hours next day digging it free. On the 21st the aircraft flew to Malta, whence it took off for Cairo very early the following morning. Three hours and 55 minutes later, at 0650hrs, they crossed the Egyptian coast near Benghazi. The rear starboard engine had to be switched off. They could maintain height on three, but set course for Alexandria, which was 130 miles (209km) nearer than their intended destination. When the second starboard engine failed four hours later, they had no choice except to put down 50 miles (80km) from Mersa Matruh. With the reduction gear of both engines broken and two tyres punctured, in the wilderness and without a wireless set, they were forlorn. Presently, however, their *deus ex machina* – or, rather, three camel-borne *dei* – materialised. Money changed hands and the nomads rode away to summon help. It arrived the following afternoon from Aboukir. Repairs were done and the aircraft made the short hop to Heliopolis after having being marooned for ten days.

On 8 January 1919 *Old Carthusian* was once more on route at 0330hrs. After 11 hours all four engines gave signs of fuel starvation. Cleaning the filters made some improvement but they again lost an engine and had to set down at Abu Kemal shortly before 1300hrs. Some 90 minutes later the exasperated crew and passengers were in the air once more; but a storm forced them down in the desert, where they spent the night 110 miles (177km) from Baghdad. January 11 saw them on

their way to Ahwaz, in Persia. From there the next leg was to Bandar Abbas, which they reached on the 12th. On the 13th they departed for Karachi. They were flying along the west coast of India, three miles (5km) offshore, when they yet again had to cut an engine. At Ormara, a fishing village 170 miles (273km) from Karachi, they landed. Luckily there was a telegraph station there and a bungalow rest house for visiting officials of the Indian Civil Service, and the Political and Posts and Telegraph Services. Signals were sent to Karachi and Cairo and a comfortable night was passed in the rest house. To enable the cantankerous *Old Carthusian* to take off on three engines, the air crew and NCOs removed everything possible from the aircraft and drained all but 220 gallons (1,000 litres) of petrol. To compound their difficulties, McEwen had sunstroke from sitting in the front gunner's cockpit. A gunboat, HMS *Britannia*, arrived next morning to take him and the mail aboard.

At 1745hrs the flight was resumed. With only three engines, the take-off run was a mile long and the climb to 1,000ft (305m) took 20 minutes. Then one of the three serviceable engines died. Maclaren and his crew were still 35 miles (56km) short of their final destination. The remaining two engines began to overheat, indicated air speed was down to 52mph (84km/h) and the aircraft was losing 10ft (3m) of altitude every minute. It barely cleared the hills west of Karachi. Maclaren had signalled his estimated time of arrival there, so a flarepath was lit and Very lights were fired. At 1715hrs, one month and a day since leaving England, the V1500 touched down.

British phlegm and the restraints that were customary among officers broke down as Captain and second pilot expressed their jubilation: when they emerged from the aircraft they held each other by the arms and literally danced with joy.

If they had made the long journey from England in an HP 0/400 with its two reliable Rolls-Royce 322hp Eagle engines, it would have saved half the time and avoided all the delays except those imposed by bad weather.

Their rewards were appointment as an Officer of the Order of the British Empire for Maclaren,

Below: **A Vickers Valentia the last in the line of Vimy-derived transports. Some examples were to continue in service during the early part of World War Two.** *(MOD)*

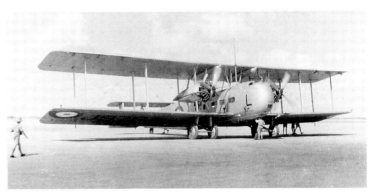

the Air Force Cross for Halley and the Air Force Medal for each of the sergeants.

The route they had established was next flown without technical hold-ups by an HP 0/400. In May the RAF began a weekly Cairo to Karachi service, shared by two HP 0/400 squadrons. The Air Ministry claimed that this would give crews valuable experience in the event of any emergency which demanded the rapid transport of troops. To demonstrate the speed with which such airlifts could be organised and carried out, a six-month exercise involving three squadrons and 51 HP 0/400s operating between England and Egypt began in April. Eight men were killed and 15 aircraft wrecked in accidents, which prejudiced a regular air service between Britain and India. It was agreed, however, to supply Iraq from Egypt by air instead of by sea.

Pilots, who also had to be competent navigators, joined the RAF from a love of flying and to defend their country in the event of another war. They had not relished the unmilitary task of carrying mails during the early peacetime months instead of training for the next time they went into action: which, as guardians of dominions that covered a greater part of the world than any other country's, they might have to do at any time with little warning. After the expensive misfortunes during the six-month exercise, the junior Service was not only the object of the others' jealousy but was also regarded askance by the Treasury. It was ironical that a mail service offered the only acceptable reason for them to keep in practice to fly long distances.

Keeping the peace in the Middle East proved the just cause for doing so. This duty had two facets: to administer the newly acquired areas formerly ruled by Turkey; and to run a scheduled transport operation between Baghdad and Cairo for RAF and Army personnel and cargo, and mail for the Post Office.

The First Air Evacuations

When Edmund Burke wrote in 1777 "... our ancestors have changed a savage wilderness into a glorious empire", Britain's territorial possessions had spread only over parts of India, North America and the Caribbean, while Gibraltar was also under the British flag. All had brought conflict. With the end of the Great War in 1918 came more responsibilities and trouble in parts of the Middle East that were as savage as anywhere Britain ruled in Asia or Africa.

These territories and populations newly under British mandate were small, but their peoples were fierce and internecine fighting had been endemic for centuries. It was difficult to perceive anything that Burke's dithyrambics could justly describe as

glorious additions to the British Empire. For the RAF, however, they became an essential proving area for the use of air power. In the course of peaceable missions, as much as on belligerent sorties, the air force was learning much that would be useful in future wars or campaigns.

Turkey, in defeat, defied the armistice by clandestinely spreading sedition; most assiduously in the oil-rich province of Mosul, whose capital town had the same name. Kurdistan, homeland of the Kurds, was part of the Turkish Republic. It lay in the mountains of north-eastern Iraq on the Persian (now Iranian) frontier and its boundaries had never been clearly defined. The most persistent instigator of unrest was a Kurdish Sheikh, Mahmoud. An unrelenting enemy of Britain, his tribe had fought for Turkey in the Mesopotamian Campaign. The Turks had duly given him the governership of Sulimaniya, a province whose main town was eponymous (as were all Iraqi provincial capitals) 60 miles (96km) east of Kirkuk in south-eastern Kurdistan. When peace was declared (a euphemism for optimistic hopes that the tribes would abandon aggression), the British, with inadequate understanding of Mesopotamian mores in general and Mahmoud's character in particular, promoted him to be Governor of South Kurdistan. He repaid

their naiveté six months later by mounting a rebellion against the British and was removed from office. Frequent minor insurrections made Iraq a rumbling volcano of seething defiance throughout the next decade.

On occasion, Bristol Fighters and DH9s had to resume the transport role and drop supplies to besieged Army units and to ferry civilian officials out of danger. As usual in that era a gunboat was at hand, patrolling the Tigris. In September a DH9A dropping supplies for her was shot down by tribesmen's rifle fire and its crew were murdered. Incidents of this kind continued, usually without the offenders being caught.

In 1922, under Sheikh Mahmoud's influence, another Kurdish tribal chief, Kerim Fattah Beg, began to make himself notorious. The Kurds, who in the 1990s are still rebelling against Iraq, erupted into mutiny on a bigger scale than ever before. In the 1920s they numbered about 1,500,000. Many worked in Baghdad, where the men were recognisable by their dress: baggy trousers gathered at the ankle, shirt, waistcoat, small turban; and a rifle from which they were inseparable. A Kurd without a rifle was as unimaginable as a plutocratic war profiteer without a cigar.

DH9s of No 30 Sqdn were sent to Kirkuk, in

Kurdistan, which is still a source of Kurdish insurrection, but against Saddam Hussein these days. It was from there that the first large-scale evacuation of British and pro-British civilians by air was laid on.

This operation saw the debut of aircraft specifically built to carry troops, the Vickers Vernon. A variant of the Vickers Vimy bomber and Vickers commercial airliner, it entered squadron service in 1922 with two Rolls-Royce engines. In the heat of Iraq these did not develop enough power to

Above: **A Neil-Robertson casualty stretcher strapped to the rear fuselage decking of a Bristol F2B.** *(PJ)*

carry a full load in rarefied air, so were replaced by 450hp Napier Lions. It had a crew of two and seats for 12 passengers. On 19 and 20 June one Vernon took parties of civilians from Kirkuk to Baghdad. On 5 September the evacuation was continued by two Vernons, 24 DH9As and three Bristol Fighters. A Bristol could take one passenger in the rear cockpit, the DH9 two.

In the spring of 1923 an attack on Kirkuk, instigated by Mahmoud, was expected. This time it was troops whom the Vernons had to carry to safety, which was another "first". The garrison comprised Assyrian Levies, who were taken all the way by air, and Sikhs, who made the first part of the journey by train. Nos 45 and 70 Squadrons each provided five aircraft. No 45's commander was the future Air Chief Marshal Sir Arthur Harris, C-in-C Bomber Command from February 1942 until Germany surrendered in May 1945. Mahmoud's continued defiance called for drastic retribution. The first punitive act was the bombing of his base in Sulimaniya when he ignored a summons to Baghdad. His misconduct was not the only factor that the British had to address: Turkey had not withdrawn its entire force when the armistice was signed. The troops who remained in Iraq were active in aiding and abetting Mahmoud. To settle his hash once and for all and to bustle the remnants of the Turkish Army back across the frontier, an expeditionary force set out in March 1923 for Rowanduz (now Ruwandiz) in the province of Sulimaniya, 60 miles (96km) east of Mosul and 30 miles (48km) west of the Turkish border. Strategically it was important to whichever nation controlled it, for it stood on the only road to Persia, whose frontier was a mere 40 miles (64km) to the east. The Turkish frontier lay the same distance to the north, although there was no road to it. The column of British and Indian Army horse and foot plus Assyrian Levies faced a gruelling march through mountainous country.

On its way to Rowanduz the column met intermittent harassment from the mountains, where an estimated 700 Kurds and 300-odd Turks found ample cover for snipers. The column was strongly backed up by air reconnaissance and supply. In the first weeks the RAF liaison officer was able to find suitable places for Vernons to land. As the expeditionary force climbed into the mountains, supplies were dropped by parachute; and the air crews were given a taste of sniper fire. The snow began to thaw and rain to fall, which made the going increasingly arduous for the troops. A variety of rations had to be dropped to provide a diet acceptable to a religious and ethnic mixture of men, as well as clothing, boots, tobacco, soap, horseshoe nails and numerous other essentials. It was a gruelling chore for the pilots and their crews as well as for the men whom they were victualling.

In May the next year, Kirkuk was again the scene

of urgent intervention by the British. This time it was a religious quarrel between Moslems of various beliefs and Assyrians, who were now Christians. The Assyrians' recorded history goes back to 2500 BC when their country was a dependency of Babylon, but for centuries they had had no homeland of their own. Those who were shooting Moslems in the streets of Kirkuk were Levies – hence their possession of rifles. The nearest British regiment, the Royal Iniskilling Fusiliers, was in Baghdad, a distance of 150 miles (241km) and five days' travel overland. Four Vernons, which each carried 12 passengers, and the 20-seat Victoria, hurried there and a further 79 officers and men followed by air within 24 hours.

Mahmoud, whose hash in fact had by no means been settled, bobbed up again: taking advantage of the unrest in Kirkuk, he declared a holy war against the Assyrians and British. This gave the British excellent reason to bomb Sulimaniya and occupy it; but they did not catch Mahmoud.

Vernons and Victorias continued to shuttle all over Iraq and south to Egypt for the next 10 years, transporting troops, equipment, ammunition and a great variety of goods.

Throughout the decade, in the Middle East and

India, co-operation between the RAF and Army improved as the latter relied increasingly on air drops for supplies to large columns on the march against insurgents. This did not necessarily ameliorate all aspects of inter-Service relationship. In many ways the RAF was resented by the other two, who would have preferred to have their own air arms and were not backward in making suggestions about how the junior Service should do its job. The Navy did have a few aircraft, but only for torpedo dropping and reconnaissance.

In Afghanistan the tribes were as fractious and bloodthirsty as they have shown themselves to be in the 1990s. In November and December 1928 three of the biggest tribes rebelled against the King, Amanullah. Amid the widespread rioting and slaughter the road to India was blocked. In Kabul, the capital, the British Legation's only means of communication now with the Indian Government and Army Headquarters was through the local wireless station. On 5 December the British Minister, Sir Francis Humphrys, signalled the Air Officer Commanding India, Air Vice Marshal Sir Geoffrey Salmond, to warn him that he might have to request air evacuation of British subjects. On 17

December he sent a message asking for the women and children to be evacuated immediately, but it was cut off before the transmission was completed.

In August 1926 No 70 Sqdn in Iraq and No 216 in Egypt were the first to receive a new troop-carrier, the Vickers Victoria. With a two-man crew and twin 570hp Napier Lion engines, it carried 22 passengers. One of 70 Sqdn's Victorias was detailed for the evacuation task. It left Hinaidi, the RAF station 6 miles (9.6km) east of Baghdad, on 16 December and reached Karachi a day later.

Fighting in Afghanistan continued, but on the 22nd the Kabul wireless station was on the air again and on the morrow the airlift began, augmented by three DH9As to carry luggage. That day, the Victoria flew 21 women and children, of whom only seven were British, to Risalpur, while the two-seaters carried 390lb (177kg) of baggage. On the 24th the Victoria fetched 17 passengers, nearly all German or French, and 11 DH9As brought out one each. Salmond's personal aircraft, a Hinaidi, happened to be grounded at the airfield after which it was named, when the evacuation had been requested, but returned to India in time to give a hand three days before Christmas. A heavy night bomber with a crew

Above: **Two Vickers Victoria VI's of No 216 Squadron RAF stationed in Egypt. The aircraft shown are powered by two 440 hp Bristol Jupiter nine-cylinder air-cooled radial engines. Victoria's were used to great effect in the evacuation of Kabul.** *(PJ)*

of four and two 440hp Bristol Jupiter VIII engines, it could carry 6,440lb (2,921kg). By New Year's Day 1929 all the women and children from the European legations, as well as other passengers, had been flown to safety.

Fighting between the loyal forces and rebels had become so fierce and widespread that, at this point, a pause was forced on the evacuation. Amanullah abdicated and the conflict abated. He and his family were flown out. The last phase of the emergency mission began on 29 January. More aircraft were needed. Seven of No 70 Sqdn's Victorias and the AOC's Hinaidi resumed the job and finished it on 25 February. The British Minister was aboard the last one to leave. In those two months and two days 586 passengers and 24,000lb (10,886kg) of cargo had been transported.

The task had been made immensely difficult by the intense cold, which affected engines when having to take off at 5,900ft (1,800m) altitude where the air is thin, and by the height of the surrounding mountains. King George V sent his congratulations.

Logistical requirements had had priority during the war, but another use for aircraft apart from the primary one of attacking the enemy was not neglected. Casualties had always engaged the attention of the General Staff and commanders in the field at all levels from Field Marshal to subaltern. This was not only from humanitarian, but also practical, concern. The more quickly wounded men could be given medical treatment, the more lives could be saved. The odds were better on their recovery and continued usefulness, even if only in rear echelons. If they were fully restored, the sooner they would be back in the battle line. The trench warfare on the Western Front gave no scope for moving them to hospital by air.

The first opportunity came in 1920, when an expeditionary force was sent to British Somaliland (now Somalia). Military action was provoked by the rebellious leader of the Dervishes, a Moslem sect. His polysyllabic name, Mohammed bin Abdulla Hassan, had been disrespectfully modified in the British press to The "Mad Mullah". He had been carrying on his campaign against subjection to the British – reasonably enough – for 17 years and was now about to be given his come-uppance.

The RAF element comprised 12 DH9As. Wing Commander W. Tyrrell, Senior Medical Officer, arranged for one more to be added and converted to carry two patients: one on a stretcher in the fuselage, the other seated in the rear cockpit. The column opened hostilities on 20 January and the cease-fire was ordered three weeks later. The ambulance aircraft was called on eight times. The first patient was an officer dangerously ill with septicaemia and a high temperature. He was taken 160 miles by motor ambulance to the nearest airstrip and flown 75 miles (120km) to a field hospital,

operated on, then flown to a base hospital. The seven other patients were also suffering from ailments, not wounds. During the same period, at Abu Kemal, in Syria, 2,000 miles (3,220km) to the north and 260 miles (420km) west-north-west of Baghdad, a small British contingent was besieged by the usual disaffected Arabs who resented British suzerainty. The RAF component was still flying the RE8, which had begun its career in 1916. An Army officer was badly wounded. The doctor had a car seat put in the rear cockpit for this patient, who was flown to Hinaidi.

A year and eight months later another improvised casualty airlift was flown. Flying at low level on reconnaissance for an Army column, the pilot of a DH.9A was wounded by ground fire. He made a forced landing in which both he and his air gunner were badly injured. Two aircraft of the same squadron, which had arrived to join the column, took them to hospital. The injured men would normally have been given a ride in the rear cockpit; but this would mean that the air gunners, who were aircraftmen, not officers or sergeants, would have had to stay behind. Rations on these expeditions were always meagre, so it would be unfair to expect the Army to feed them. Therefore they volunteered to be roped to the lower mainplane of his aircraft and in this uncomfortable, precarious way they were flown back to base.

Throughout the 1920s DH9As, Bristol Fighters and Vernons made casualty evacuation flights. An improvisation for the first two of these types that was much used during that decade was the attachment of a light stretcher to the upper fuselage, astern of the pilot's cockpit. Even patients who were fresh-air buffs must have wished that somebody would think of a less exposed alternative. Someone did in 1931. In 1927 No 84 Sqdn in Iraq had received the first Mark I Westland Wapiti. The Mk II of 1930 was the first of all-metal construction. The latest, Mk IIA, had a Bristol Jupiter VIII engine of 550hp. The stretcher was now fitted inside the fuselage. These versatile aircraft had already been used for bombing, reconnaissance and as escorts to the Victorias that carried out the evacuation from Kabul. Even their name was unconventional. It was the custom in the RAF to christen aeroplanes alliteratively with the maker's name. All but this one's were easily pronounceable and familiar. Wapiti is a Red Indian word for a species of deer; and the uninitiated put the emphasis on the second syllable instead of the first.

In 1929 two Victorias made the first international ambulance flight when they evacuated 13 patients from Iraq to India. The Quetta earthquake in 1935 and military activities on the North-West Frontier caused a plethora of casualties in India. The total number evacuated by air exceeded the figure for the Middle East.

The squadrons and other RAF units serving in the Middle East from November 1918 for the next two decades continued to gain the valuable experience that only active service can bestow. John Milton's observation, "For what can war but endless war still breed?" was prophetically apposite for Britain in the history of the first 45 years of the 20th century. "Bomber" Harris, who rose to be Marshal of the Royal Air Force and a peer, was not the only future Air Officer who commanded a squadron, a flight or was of a lower rank in those minor campaigns. Others who, in RAF parlance, "got their knees brown" in that troublesome part of Asia were Air Marshal Sir Basil Embry, Air Marshal the Hon Sir Ralph Cochrane, Air Chief Marshal Sir Hugh Dowding, Air Marshal Sir Robert Saundby, Air Marshal Sir Roderic Hill, Air Marshal Sir Alan Lees; and Air Commodore Raymond Collishaw, who had 60 victories as a fighter pilot in the Great War and, from the declaration of the new war in 1939 until July 1941, commanded the formation that became Desert Air Force in North Africa.

RAF transport squadrons had extended their range when, in 1931, seditious riots and demands for rule by Greece rocked the Crown Colony of Cyprus. On 23 October 1931 seven Victorias of 261 Sqdn, stationed at Heliopolis, in Egypt, fetched a company of the King's Regiment, based at Ramle, 10 miles south (16km) of Tel Aviv in Palestine (now Israel), to the island. The 126 officers and men, plus 23 ground staff airmen to service the aeroplanes and maintain wireless contact with Egypt and Palestine, were the first to be flown over the sea. Although the crossing was only 200 miles (320km), in an era when flying was a rare experience and even the most meticulously maintained engines were liable to falter, the soldiers perhaps felt a certain uneasiness; all the more because it is doubtful that they were issued with life jackets.

An annual event for the British and Indian Armies in India was the Chitral Relief, when the British and Indian troops stationed at that desolate outpost of empire on the North-West Frontier changed places with a relief force of men and mules that took 36 days to march there. In 1930 when the column was delayed by difficulties of the terrain, supplies were delivered by parachute.

Six years later the relieving battalion of the 3/11 Sikhs was to travel by motor transport and aeroplane. Only two Valentias were available to carry out the airlift from Risalpur in West Punjab, now in Pakistan, to Chitral's airfield, Drosh. Together they had room for only half a company (two platoons). At Headquarters some Staff officers thought that the troops would be reluctant to be flown. On the contrary, there was intense competition among them for a place. The Granthi (Sikh priest) was among them, carrying their religion's holy book, the Granth Sahib. There was also anxiety at HQ about the safety aspect. The Valentia's ceiling was 17,000ft (5,180m), but fully loaded and fuelled, at the temperature prevailing, its performance fell a couple of thousand feet below this. They had to fly at 10,000ft (3,050m) through the Lowri Pass with 14,000ft (4,270m) mountain ranges on either side. The mission was safely accomplished. In 1938 the same route was flown. This time the Valentias conveyed 288 troops and 14.5 tons of gear. While these operations were being carried out there were other troop movements by surface and air in the North-West Frontier Province. Altogether nearly 6,000 officers and other ranks and 400 tons of cargo were flown. This constituted the biggest pre-Second World War military transportation.

Both medical evacuation and trooping by air were firmly established by 3 September 1939, when Britain declared war on Germany, and Royal Air Force transport squadrons were to be tested even further.

Above: **Only four Avro 561 Andover transports were built. All examples were powered by a single 600 hp Rolls-Royce Condor IIIa engine. The aircraft shown first flew in 1924 and was subsequently used in air ambulance trials. Andovers did not enter service with the RAF, but J7261 ended life as a development aircraft at AE&A establishment Martlesham Heath Suffolk.** *(BR)*

CHAPTER THREE

Airborne Forces

To penetrate a beachhead needed shock troops of some kind,
highly mobile and positioned to attack the enemy from the rear.
Parachute and gliderborne troops met the requirements.

Parachutes were not a recent invention. People had long been attracted by the notion of floating from a great height to the ground, gently and under control. Leonardo da Vinci (1453–1519) designed one, but, like the flying machines he sketched, none was made. In the late eighteenth and early nineteenth centuries parachutists were fairground turns and jumps had been made from captive balloons. The first person to parachute out of an aircraft was also the first to fly inverted and perform rolls and both positive and negative G loops: a Frenchman, Adolphe Pégoud, in 1913.

The military use of parachutes – but forbidden to aircrew – began in 1914 and continued through-out the Great War. On both sides, observers in the baskets of tethered observation balloons used them for jumping to safety when aeroplanes attacked them. German pilots were allowed parachutes from early 1918. The innovation in the 1930s was to drop soldiers by parachute in large numbers. The drawbacks were twofold: that they would be lightly armed, and conditions would not always enable them to assemble quickly after landing. Far-sighted military planners recognised that well-entrenched defenders against an attack from the sea could hold out until a frustrated enemy withdrew. To penetrate a beachhead needed shock troops of some kind, highly mobile and positioned to attack the enemy from the rear. Parachute and gliderborne troops met the requirements.

France had been ignored for decades as an ardent sponsor of parachute development. With the advent of aeroplanes she offered prizes for improvements to parachutes, the major purpose being to arrive at one that pilots could wear. No other country showed as much interest.

Another distinction, the details of which have become obscured with the lapse of time, is that two French officers made the first offensive parachute drop when, in 1918, they parachuted behind enemy lines with explosives to destroy the Germans' communications.

Andrei Nikolaevich Tupolev was the first great Russian designer of aircraft. His G1, a variant of his TB-1 (ANT-4) twin-engine bomber, was the first Soviet military transport and made its maiden flight on 26 November 1925. In December 1930 the four-engine TB-3 (ANT-6) flew for the first time and in 1932 its military transport variant, the G2, appeared.

On the eve of the Second World War three countries had formed a new arm – paratroops. This meant special training for the air force as well as the army personnel involved. It is significant that all these countries, Germany, Russia and Italy, were dictatorships avid for colonial expansion and European or world dominance, political and military.

Their common factors were allegedly patriotism, but commercial greed, lust for power and the egotism of their leaders, who craved fame, were the real motivators. All empires have been created for the same reasons, including the British. The wars of the Crusaders and Islam were exceptions, motivated

by religious bigotry. There was a touch of lunacy, too, about the regimes that first fostered military parachuting: Hitler was undoubtedly certifiable; only a lunatic could have had so many political and military suspects executed as Stalin did; and Mussolini, like every demagogue, was clearly insane with delusions of grandeur.

There was also a significant contrast in the characters of the nations that were pioneers in the new tactic of assault by paratroops. German soldiers had a reputation for bravery and efficiency. The general perception of Russian soldiers was of ruthless men who fought with great tenacity because death could not be worse than the bleak lives their national economy compelled them to endure. Italian soldiers were ridiculed as timid by people who have never been in action against anyone and by most of those who fought them. However, members of Allied infantry and armoured regiments who opposed Italian paratroops in North Africa will tell you that most were first class. Yet the public image of Italian soldiers is of reluctant fighters prone to panic and surrender. This is the legacy of the Battle of Caporetto in October and November 1917, when the Italian Army lost 200,000 men, retreated in panic and lost a great area of their country to the attacking Germans and Austrians. Their detractors would be astonished to learn that the first parachute unit in history was Italian. It comprised only one company, but was formed as early as 1928. The next was Russian the following year.

By 1931 the Soviet Union had trained a battalion, equipped with four-engine TB-3s. In 1934 the Russian Army staged a demonstration by an entire regiment of 1,500 men at which the military attachés of every country with an embassy in Moscow were present. Britain's was Field Marshal Lord Wavell, then a Major-General. He was not enthusiastic about the concept of dropping parachutists to take the enemy in the rear and critical also of the length of time it took for an attacking force to muster after being widely scattered. The obvious advantages and potential for improvement appear not to have occurred to him.

TB-3s had a fixed undercarriage with long legs. On an exercise in 1935 they carried light tanks or artillery between these. The following year saw two events that should have been a stark warning to the world's other great powers. First, a whole brigade was transported from Moscow to Vladivostock by these aircraft. Next, a battalion of paratroops was flown 100 miles (160km) in 200 converted bombers and did a night drop. Both events were witnessed by British, German and other military observers. That should have given Wavell and the other two-star intellectuals something to think about.

A further Russian innovation was the military glider. In the 1930s there were three types of these, the five-passenger G4, the eight-passenger A7 and 18-passenger G31. Gliders' advantages over troop-carrying aeroplanes were that they were silent and could all be landed close together. The first effective glider had been made and flown by a German, Otto Lilienthal, in 1893. In 1896 he crashed one

Above: **Russian paratroopers tumble from the overwing door of a Tupolev TB-3. Originally designed as a heavy bomber the TB-3 was used as a transport in World War Two serving in that role until 1944. This large air-craft; wingspan 132 ft 10 in (40.5 m) was powered by four 730 hp M-17 V-12 liquid-cooled engines. Later versions were powered by M-34R or M-34RN/RNF engines with horsepower increased to 900/1280 hp.** *(BR)*

and was killed. After the First World War the Allies forbade Germany an air force, but allowed aircraft production to continue and a national airline, Lufthansa, to be set up. In 1920 a gliding club, the Deutscher Luftsportverband (German Air Sport Association) was created and by 1930 had 50,000 members. In 1926 Germany made a clandestine arrangement with the USSR to train Lufthansa crews and members of the gliding club in military aviation in Russia.

Still there was no move by the British War Office or Air Ministry towards creating any type of airborne force. In Germany, however, not only were paratroops and aircraft ready for action by 1938, but also gliders, DFS230s, had been built to carry assault troops. A whole division was being trained for two purposes, to make parachute drops or to be landed by gliders towed by aeroplanes.

Paratroops were dropped in war for the first time when Russia invaded Finland on 30 November 1939. On 29 September a Soviet-German Treaty of Friendship had been signed when Germany and Russia agreed on how they would partition Poland between them. Several small groups of Russian paratroops were dropped on the Finnish side of the Russian frontier with the intention of joining together. None succeeded in doing so, most of them lost their way and the Finns either killed or captured them all.

The first properly planned and executed paratroop and gliderborne assaults were made on Norway and Denmark at dawn on 9 April 1940. In February Winston Churchill had addressed an audience of Scandinavian journalists with the words: "I could not reproach Denmark if she surrendered to Nazi attack. The other two Scandinavian countries, Norway and Sweden, have at least a ditch over which they can feed the tiger, but Denmark is so terribly near Germany that it would be impossible to bring help. Personally, I would in any case not undertake to guarantee Denmark." Striving for a metaphor, he misrepresented the dilemma. The friendly act of feeding a wild animal that metaphorically represented the enemy was the very opposite of the Danes' attitude. They bravely had no truck with Hitler.

The air component for the invasion consisted of 500 transport aeroplanes, mostly the Junkers Ju 52/3m. There were also four-engine transports, the Ju 90 version of an airliner, and the Focke-Wulf Condor, essentially a reconnaissance bomber. Do 24 and Do 26 flying boats also took part in the rape of Norway. The paratroops' objectives were the main airfields in both countries. Copenhagen fell in twelve hours, which meant defeat for the whole of that small country. Norway, 1,200 miles long and mountainous, held out until 9 June even though Oslo had fallen on 9 April, invasion day, when the Germans landed by air and sea. A second paratroop drop on the 14th proved disastrous for the invaders. The purpose was to seize a narrow pass in the mountains through which the Norwegian Army would pass on its way northward. The fly-in was so low that several Germans were killed because their parachutes did not have time to open, and the rest were captured.

Germany delivered a total of 30,000 men, 2,350 tons of supplies and 250,000 gallons (1,136,500 litres) of petrol and oil by air. The aircraft, which also carried the paratroops and towed the gliders, was the Ju 52/3m. This aeroplane holds the same high place in the esteem, indeed the hagiology, of flying as the Douglas DC-3 Dakota. Neither the

aviation industry nor the Luftwaffe gave names to aircraft, but to the air crews and the airborne troops who were passengers in, or were towed by, the Ju 52 (as it has always been called), it was "Tante [Aunt] Ju". It could carry 18 fully equipped paratroops, had a maximum speed of 180mph (290km/h) and 808 miles (1,300km) range.

Above: **In flight refuelling in 1929. The upper aircraft is a Douglas C-1, the other is a Fokker C-2 trimotor.** *(HG)*

On 10 May 1940 Germany launched its attack on the Low Countries. General Kurt Student set a dubious example to other commanders of his rank by jumping with the first wave. This was a magnificent display of leadership but not of generalship: when the Dutch resisted so much more successfully than expected, he should have been at his headquarters, directing the battle. The glider-borne troops went into action against Holland and Belgium aboard 45 DFS230s, towed by Ju 52s. Altogether 475 of the latter took part in the invasion. Paratroops landed at Rotterdam and deep inside Holland, but met a retaliation for which they had not bargained. The plan was for small paratroop drops to capture the airfields, followed by air-landed troops who would in turn be backed up quickly by conventional ground forces. The Dutch, aware of what had happened in Scandinavia, had deployed their army differently from the way Student expected. Instead of positioning it in strength to defend the frontier, they placed a strong defence around the airfields. The assault cost the enemy heavy casualties. An interesting tactic by the attackers was the use of 12 floatplanes to land 120 troops at Rotterdam to capture a bridge.

In Belgium, gliders landed on top of Fort Eben Emael, on the German border. Only 72 men were needed. The sound of aircraft engines would have alerted the defenders. The invaders arrived silently at dawn, their gliders having been released at 8,000ft (2,440m) before crossing the Belgian frontier, and held their position for more than 24 hours until conventional reinforcements arrived. Their casualties were only six killed and 20 wounded.

The Ju 52/3m was first operated in 1932 as an

Above: **Fokker Universal of 1924 was one of a large number of different types trialed by the United States Army.** *(JM)*

Above right: **A Fairchild C-8 transport fitted with floats.** *(JM)*

Right: **US Army Fairchild C-31 single-engined transport fitted with retractable undercarriage.** *(JM)*

Above: **Ex-KLM Fokker F.XXII and F.XXXVI in RAF service, Prestwick, 1940.** *(BR)*

airliner with seats for 15 to 17 passengers. This three-engine workhorse constituted 75 per cent of the German Lufthansa fleet and was bought by several foreign operators. In 1935 a bomber variant, Ju 53m g3e, began to equip the Luftwaffe's first bomber squadrons. In the Spanish Civil War of 1936–39 it flew missions for the Nationalist (Fascist) Air Force and for the German Legion Kondor, a Luftwaffe component that Hitler sent to the aid of his fellow dictator, General Franco. Germany further

ambulance, freighter, and detonater of magnetic mines. Production continued until 1952. Its engines were successively 600hp, 725hp and 830hp BMW, 925hp Bristol Pegasus, 750hp ENMASA, 710hp Wright Cyclone, Jumo 5 diesel, Jumo 206 and BMW VI.

Italy also helped Franco by transporting troops in the Savoia-Marchetti SM81, which had come into military use in 1935 as both transport and bomber, variants of an airliner. Another tri-motor type, in its air force version it had 700hp Piaggio, 580hp Alfa Romeo, or 1000 Gnome-Rhne engines. The SM82 was a purpose-designed transport that followed it from the same factory. Its three 950hp Alfa Romeo engines enabled it to carry 40 troops; and, on one occasion, 96. It was used in the world's first major campaign in which troop transport aircraft figured: 320 such machines, 75 per cent of them bomber/transports, carried troops and made supply drops in Abyssinia.

An earlier dual purpose transport and bomber, the Caproni Ca.133 of 1932, was specially built for duty in Italy's African colonies and powered by three 450/460hp Piaggios. In 1938 the Ca.310 transport appeared, with two Piaggio 470hp engines. Italy's biggest transport, of which there was a bomber variant, was the Piaggio .108, with four 1500 Piaggio engines; it entered service in 1941.

In the administration of parachute and glider-borne troops, Germany showed greater wisdom than other nations. General Kurt Student, the first commander of the Airborne Division, had been a pilot in the First World War and rejoined the German Military Air Service when it was re-formed as the Luftwaffe. Because airborne troops depended on the air force for transport, the airborne branch was made part of the Luftwaffe (as the anti-aircraft artillery and searchlight regiments were). This avoided the usual inter-Service pettiness and obstructionism that exists in all nations. What the airborne troops needed in the way of aircraft, they got without argument, because the air crews and their passengers belonged to the same service.

In the British Army and RAF the traditional and natural prejudice in favour of one's own arm would create the friction that Reichsmarshall Hermann Goering had avoided by putting all the requirements for the Airborne Division under the orders of one man. The moment for the introduction of paratroops to the British forces had not yet arrived, however.

In France, the Royal Navy's evacuation of the British Expeditionary Force and soldiers, sailors and airmen of Allied countries, mainly from Dunkirk, began on 26 May 1940.

Churchill had become Prime Minister on 11 May. On 22 June he issued a memorandum calling for 5,000 paratroops to begin training at once. This, naturally, although welcomed by those who

helped Franco by lending him 20 of the transport variant to carry 13,500 Moroccan soldiers and 300 tons of freight from Tetuan, in Spanish Morocco, to Seville.

Other uses were as casualty evacuation

Left: **A Caproni Ca-101 transport, which also served as a bomber and reconnaissance aircraft, was developed into the Ca-111 and later the Ca-133. All were powered by three Piaggio or Alfa Romeo radial engines and saw service up until Italy's surrender in 1943.** *(BR)*

Below: **Built for the French Air Force the Candron CA45 Goëland was powered by two six-cylinder Renault Bengali air-cooled engines. Many were pressed into Luftwaffe service after the surrender of France.** *(BR)*

volunteered, was not in general well received by the Army, whose regiments were reluctant to part with any of their best men: those who had the courage and enterprise to come forward at once to join the new arm. Nor was it a cause for jubilation in the RAF: lack of aircraft and aircrew and concentration on the manufacture of fighters to defend the British Isles left the Air Ministry poorly placed for providing aeroplanes for soldiers to jump out of.

In Britain, training paratroops was a rough and ready business. The Parachute Training School was at Ringway, which is now Manchester Airport. The instructors were members of the RAF Physical Training Branch. Whitley bombers were being

withdrawn from service, so six were given to the school. The rear turret was removed and a wooden platform built at the tail of the aircraft. Pupils stood there, pulled the parachute's ripcord and were dragged into space by the slipstream. Later, this method of exit was changed. A hole 3 feet (1m) in diameter was cut in the floor. Beneath it was a cylinder like a dustbin with its lid off and bottom removed. This was to protect the tailplane and elevators against a man being blown against them, rather than to protect the man from being damaged by the tail unit. Their many pupils bashed their faces against this tube. There were many deaths and injuries among

both pupils and instructors, mostly through parachutes failing to open.

On 10 February 1941 the first British paratroop operation was carried out. The target was the Tragino Aqueduct in southern Italy. The paratroops were 36 members of X Troop, 11th Special Air Service Battalion. The aircraft were three Whitleys of No 51 Squadron and three of No 78. They flew to Malta on the night of 7–8 February and took off on the attack in darkness on the 10th. They dropped their passengers from 300ft (100m) in a steep-sided valley from which they barely managed to climb out. One aircraft went down and the crew were captured. The aqueduct was blown up, but the submarine that was to take the paratroops home failed to show up and they were taken prisoner.

The second brilliant coup by the British Army's Parachute Regiment followed a year later. Anyone who saw Charles Cox in civilian clothes before the war might have mistaken him for a jockey: slight, with the sharp, intelligent and energetic air of a champion rider on the flat. This was more than a trifle wide of the mark, for he earned his living as a cinema projectionist and in the RAF was a radar mechanic. He had reached the rank of flight sergeant by the time he was summoned to the Air Ministry without explanation early in 1942. An air commodore who interviewed him mistakenly supposed he had volunteered for a dangerous mission. This was the first that Flight Sergeant (later Warrant Officer) Cox had heard of it and the air commodore did not explain what the venture entailed, but did say that if he volunteered he would have a fair chance of survival. Cox's promotion had been exceptionally rapid, so ... *noblesse oblige* – he accepted.

He was told nothing about the forthcoming operation but was sent on a parachute course, which imposed a severe strain on his character. He did not like it a bit, but persevered and after jumps by day and night from a tethered balloon and a Whitley, he joined a group of paratroops. Among them was a captain in the Parachute Field Engineers, who showed him an array of British radar components that Cox had to identify for him. On the night of 27 February 1942 the party boarded 12 Whitleys, six passengers in each. Only then was the flight

Bottom left: **The Lockheed XLR20-1 prototype for the US Navy. Almost identical to the US Army's C-35 and 36 (civilian model 10A) the aircraft was designed as a high speed transport. Powered by two 400/450 hp Pratt & Whitney Wasp Junior or Twin Wasp air-cooled radial engines the aircraft had a top speed of 200 mph and a range of 660-925 miles at a cruising speed of 150 mph.** *(JM)*

Below: **The American Fokker built YIC-14 transport prototype.** *(JM)*

to wear a qualified paratrooper's wings and found this an embarrassment: ignorant aggressive soldiery would challenge his right to the badge.

What he did not know until long after was that throughout their time ashore a paratrooper had covered him with a revolver: ready to shoot him dead if he were about to be captured, to ensure that he would divulge no information about British radar under torture.

On 4 April 1939 Britain had guaranteed Greece against Germany and Italy. On 28 October 1940 Mussolini, the Italian dictator, decided to attack Greece and issued an ultimatum that was to expire at dawn. With characteristic rascality he launched his invasion hours before the expiration. Churchill offered help to Greece, which the Greek Government declined on the grounds that this would provoke Germany, Italy's ally, to join in the attack. Eventually, on 7 March 1941, the first contingent of a British and Commonwealth force of 50,000 and a few RAF bomber and fighter squadrons arrived in Greece from North Africa.

On 6 April Germany did go to rescue the Italians, who were being beaten. The greatly outnumbered British, Australian and New Zealand troops were forced to retreat. Hitler ordered the occupation of the Isthmus of Corinth and the capture of the bridge over the Corinth Canal that they would have to cross. This was done by air and gave the air transport arm useful experience in the use of freight gliders. The assault force took off from the airfield at Larissa, in central Greece. Each wave of Ju 52s could lift two battalions at a time and tow the assault platoon's gliders. The retreating troops lost 12,000 men and the remainder were taken to Crete by sea. On 24 April they had to start evacuating to the island of Crete.

On 20 May the German assault on Crete began. This invasion was intended to be the first ever made entirely from the air: 500 aeroplanes, some of which carried troops, others supplies, and 70 gliders were used. At 0800hrs on 20 May, 3,000 German paratroops were dropped. By dusk their number had been more than doubled. Eventually a total of 22,250 descended on the island by parachute, Ju 52 and glider. The airlift was made in relays, accompanied by 400 bombers and 200 escorting fighters. The plan had been for paratroops to capture the airfields after the defenders had been heavily bombed, and for gliderborne troops to land on them. It did not work out like that. The defence was far fiercer than expected and inflicted heavier casualties than had been bargained for; the terrain also caused casualties. The gliders that did make it onto airfields met heavy fire.

Coordination of the attack broke down and the invasion that was planned to be made wholly by air had to be salvaged by bombing and sinking the British ships in harbour and close inshore, in the

sergeant, who was aboard the sixth one in order of take-off, told that they were all going to Bruneval, on the north coast of France. There, he was to dismantle a German radar installation and the party would bring as many parts as possible back to Britain.

When they crossed the French coast flak opened up. They made their jumps and assembled a couple of hundred yards from their objective. Some of the paras set off for a nearby copse. There was small arms fire while Cox was busy with his task, helped by the engineer captain, bullets whipping past. Presently lights were seen on the road and Major (later Major-General) John Frost, in command, thinking that enemy reinforcements were arriving, ordered the withdrawal. Helped by a couple of the paras, Cox and the engineer captain lugged the dismantled parts of the radar to the beach, once more under fire. In response to Very lights fired by Frost, landing craft ran in and took the men and the radar parts off for the return journey home. Cox was awarded a well deserved Military Medal. He was also entitled

Left: **The proto-type of the Bristol Bombay on its maiden flight 23 June 1935. Designed to specification C.26/31 it was a large, twin-engined aircraft of all-metal construction. The Bombay could carry 24 fully-armed infantry soldiers or other loads of similar weight. It entered service in 1938 to replace Vickers Valentia's in the Middle East and India.** *(BR)*

Far left: **A production Bombay awaiting service delivery. When Italy declared war in 1940, the RAF's No 216 Bomber/Transport Squadron equipped with Bombays was the only heavy bomber squadron in the Western Desert. These aircraft were used to attack Italian forces until replaced back to their transport role, by more modern types of bomber.** *(MOD)*

Above: **Although designed as a bomber aircraft the Junkers Ju-86 was pressed into service as a transport/troop carrier. Powered by two 800/880 hp BMW 132 nine-cylinder air-cooled radial engines this E-2 variant had top speed of 202 mph and a range of 746 miles.** *(BR)*

hope that none of the defenders could be evacuated by sea.

The defenders numbered 28,600 British, Australians and New Zealanders and 10,000 Greeks. Weary after the hard fighting on the Greek mainland, now short of food and ammunition and depleted by casualties among the Army and RAF, they could not hold out and there was no possibility of reinforcements by air or sea. The Allied evacuation began on 28 May and ended on the 31st. Eventually 18,600 of the Allies were taken off, 17,000 casualties and prisoners were left and 600 escaped later.

The Germans suffered over 4,000 casualties among the paratroops on Crete and 327 in the sea. Altogether, the German casualties were over 7,000 from various services. Hitler had intended to attack Malta next, but cancelled the plan, fearing further casualties on a similar scale. Informed opinion both British and German was and remains that an invasion of Malta would have succeeded, because the RAF had so few aeroplanes there.

Although the Italians initiated the invasion of Greece, they could never overcome the defenders, whose fighting qualities were superior to theirs. Despite Italy having formed the world's first parachute force, no Italian paratroops were ever dropped into battle: they fought as ordinary infantry – but more bravely than the majority of their countrymen. Both the battalions that had been formed were used in this way: their country could not afford to arm them or build enough aircraft to carry them.

The quality of these men was displayed by a group of them who, when Italy became a co-

Above: **The De Havilland Rapide was in civilian service with many airlines before 1939. The RAF renamed the aircraft Dominie and used it as a transport/communications aircraft.** *(BR)*

Left: **The Handley Page Harrow was designed in the mid-1930's as a bomber but was obsolete in that role at the declaration of war in 1939. Harrows were subsequently deployed successfully in the transport role during World War Two.** *(MOD)*

Below: **The C-34 was the military version of the DC-2 airliner. It carried 14 passengers and a crew of two at 212 mph, powered by two 875 hp Wright Cyclone GR-1820-F52 nine-cylinder radial engines. The US Army also flew C-32 and C-33 variants, whilst the US Navy had the R2D-1.** *(BR)*

belligerent of the Allies, ventured the dangerous journey through German lines to contact the British. They were given the name F Squadron and further training in parachuting. They felt that the British paras showed a certain lack of élan because they uttered no battlecry. Even on practice jumps the Italians, as they leapt from an aeroplane, shouted "Folgore! Nembo!" ("Lightning and Thunder"). Although they never went into action as parachutists, F Squadron faught with great credit as infantry.

First Allied Glider Assaults

Mobile warfare in the North African deserts and in the sky over the Mediterranean demanded the greatest scale and variety of military trans portation

by air ever carried out until then. Both the Allied and Axis air forces and armies were heavily involved. RAF Bomber and Coastal Command squadron crews either flew themselves from England to Gibraltar and on to Egypt or Libya, or were flown by Transport Command. Fighter pilots went by sea to Freetown on the West African coast, then were flown or flew themselves to Egypt. Some air crew and all ranks in ground branches travelled by sea round the Cape of Good Hope to Suez. The Germans and Italians had to depend entirely on flying their air force and army reinforcements from Sicily and sending supplies by both air and sea.

In addition to the allied movement of supplies and the sick or wounded by Ansons, Bombays, Hudsons and Dakotas, Sunderland flying boats made daily trips between Gibraltar and England carrying passengers in all the Services. Often they were RAF

Left: **Lockheed C-36 of the US Army in service as a VIP transport. This aircraft was the military version of the Lockheed Model 10 Electra.** *(JM)*

air crew who had been shot down over France and evaded capture. Sometimes they were French, Belgian, Dutch, Polish or Czech escapees from their enemy-occupied countries seeking to join one of the allied armed forces. (The many Norwegians who evaded the Germans' vigilance came to Britain by a shorter route across the North Sea.)

There were occasions when Desert Air Force transport squadrons were directly engaged in an operation against the enemy. Probably the most audacious was given the innocuous code name of Operation Chocolate. The plan was conceived by Air Vice Marshal Arthur Coningham (later Air Marshal and knighted), Air Officer Commanding DAF. In November 1942 the Second Battle of Alamein was being fought. General Rommel's assaults had failed and he was about to withdraw, when Hitler ordered him to stand firm. The Italians were already retreating. Coningham decided to play a bold hand, as usual, and attack the enemy from their rear.

First a suitable temporary base had to be found, so on 11 November a No 21 Squadron Bombay was sent to reconnoitre a patch of desert aggrandised by the name Landing Ground 125. The pilot reported that this desolate spot was in serviceable condition and no enemy was in the vicinity. The next day 12 Hudsons of 117 Sqdn, 16 of 267 Sqdn and three of No 216 carried food, water, spare parts and ammunition to the chosen place, where they unloaded then returned to base. Two Bombays of 219 Sqdn followed; arthritic and well stricken in years, their performance was far surpassed by the types that had been rapidly developed in the hothouse of approaching warfare during the late 1930s and early 1940s; but the exigencies of the campaign made it unthinkable to pension them off yet. They carried the technicians who would service the Hurricanes that were to carry out the offensive.

On 13 November No 243 Wing, under Wing Commander Darwen, comprising 36 Hurricanes of

213, 238 and 33 Squadrons at battle strength, arrived at LG125 escorting the 31 Hudsons which were making a second trip loaded with more stores. During their three-day sojourn there the Hurricanes destroyed 130 enemy vehicles and damaged at least as many for the loss of three Hurricanes. Hudsons and Dakotas took the tents and other equipment back whence they came. Dakotas replaced 219 Sqdn's Bombays soon after this operation.

On 8 November 1942, Operation Torch, the invasion of French North Africa by the 5th Army, which comprised British and American forces, had begun. The American 509th Parachute Infantry made drops at Oran, in Algeria, and Youks Les Bains and Faid Pass in Tunisia.

The 1st Parachute Squadron, Royal Engineers, arrived at Algiers by ship four days later. The Germans were now fighting on two fronts, against

Above:
**Abandoned as a
bomber aircraft
the Handley
Page Harrow was
modified as a
pure transport.
Shown here in
that form it was
renamed the
Handley Page
Sparrow and
served in many
RAF transport
squadrons.** *(BR)*

Above: **One of the large number of civilian DC-3/DST's pressed in US military service. The aircraft were given the military designation C-38.** *(JM)*

Left: **Identical to the Army's C-32, 33 and 34 the US Navy operated the aircraft as the R2D-1.** *(HG)*

Left: **US Army troops practice unloading anti-tank artillery from Douglas C-33 transports.** *(HG)*

8th Army advancing from the east and 5th Army pushing from the west. The 3rd Battalion of the Parachute Regiment jumped from their Dakotas at Bne, to the west of Algiers. In Tunisia the 5th Army was under attack from the air by Stukas based at three airfields and the advance was halted because the invaders lacked adequate fighter cover. The Allies' plan was to disrupt the dive bombers and establish their own fighters where they could be most effective. The 1st Para Sqdn RE was ordered to land in the late afternoon on 29 November at Pont du Fahs, one of the enemy air strips, and set fire to the aircraft and motor vehicles there, the petrol and ammunition dumps and the buildings.

That day, First Parachute Brigade boarded 44 USAAF Dakotas. On the way they had a signal to say that British armoured cars had already captured Pont du Fahs, so the objective was now another airfield, at Depienne. They would be escorted by a squadron of Lockheed P-38 Lightnings from which a squadron of Spitfires would take over and cover them to the target. They flew along and beyond the Atlas Mountains and were dropped onto a ploughed field. About 20 of them suffered sprains or concussion and one man was killed when his parachute did not open. Five days of hard fighting against infantry and tanks, which they won, ensued.

The Horsa, designed and manufactured by

Left: **Savoia-Marchetti SM81, three-engined transport of the Italian Air Force** *(BR)*

Bottom left: **Fresh from the factory a Douglas RD2-1 of the US Marine Corps. Note the same designation as the US Navy.** *(HG)*

Below: **First all-metal design from De Havilland, the Flamingo. This is the prototype G-AFUE in service with No 24 Squadron RAF as a transport aircraft.** *(BR)*

Airspeed, was the RAF's first operational troop-carrying glider; 3,655 were built. The MkII carried a pilot and 25 troops. Its dimensions were: span 88ft (26.8m), length 67ft (20.4m), height 19ft 6ins (5.94m), empty weight 7,500lb (3,402kg), loaded weight 15,250lb (6,917kg), gliding speed 100mph 160km/h). Glider towing was not a simple matter for either the pilot of the aeroplane or of the glider. On take-off the glider became airborne before its tug and had to be held down level with the runway to enable both to climb from the airfield. There were two possible relative positions of both aircraft. In the low-two position the aeroplane was below the tug; in the high-two position, from which the tug would be released, the aeroplane was the higher by 20ft (6.1m). Changing positions meant that the glider had to pass through the tug's slipstream, which occasioned heavy handling of control stick and rudder by the glider pilot. If this was not done properly, the glider would yaw and its pilot would receive some pithy advice in his headphones from the pilot of the tug. If the towrope broke, which was not rare, it could slash towards the glider, damage it and perhaps maim or kill its pilot.

Glider pilots had to master many skills, for there was more than one way in which they had to be able to land their aircraft, depending on the terrain and the landing space: spot landings, steep approaches, high-speed ones without using flaps, instrument flying and night flying.

Getting the Horsas to North Africa in the first place had been a fine feat of airmanship. The only way to do it was by air. No 38 Wing had carried out the movement, mostly by 295 Squadron's Halifaxes. The hazards of a night flight towing a glider were unacceptable, so they had to be brought by day along a route that passed within 100 miles (160km) of enemy air bases in south-west France. They flew at 500ft (152m) to be below the coast radar. This added the risk of a ditching for both if an engine failed or for the glider if the tow had to be cast off. Of 30 Horsas, 27 had been fetched to their destination by 7 July. One Halifax was shot down by a Focke-Wulf Condor and the Horsa it was towing alighted at sea. The three glider pilots aboard were adrift in a dinghy for eleven days before being rescued. Another was picked up after 10 hours in a dinghy when his tow rope broke.

Above: **Boeing's 247 monoplane of 1932 revolutionised fast air transport. The 247-D model was adopted by the US Air Transport Command, as a transport/crew trainer, as the C-73.** *(BR)*

Left: **First flown in 1938 the Douglas DC-5 Airliner was not used extensively by civil companies due to the demand for military transports. Production aircraft were supplied to the US Navy and US Marine Corps as the R3D-1; a 16 passenger transport and the R3D-2 mixed passenger/freighter.** *(HG)*

Above: **Such was the demand for air transport at the outbreak of war, obsolete types were pressed into service. This Armstrong Whitworth AW XV Atalanta was originally flown in the Middle East, Far East and Africa on Imperial Airways services. The aircraft, one of that fleet, is painted in RAF markings and is flying over Egypt. In civilian guise the aircraft was VT-AEG and named Aurora.**
(MOD)

The American Waco Hadrian, a Waco Aircraft Co product, was the first glider ever – and in RAF markings, at that – to be towed across the Atlantic, by an RAF Dakota. It was less strongly built than British gliders, with a fuselage of tubular steel and wood. It had a crew of two and could carry only 13 passengers, or a jeep and four men. Its span was 83ft 8in (25.5m), length 48ft 4in (14.7m), empty weight 3,750lb (1,701kg), loaded weight 8,000lb (3,628kg), towing speed 125mph (201km/h). The Sicilian operation was the only one on which the RAF towed them.

On the night of 9/10 July the invasion of Sicily, Operation Husky went in, the largest assault yet by Allied airborne troops. For half an hour in the late evening of the 9th the 1st Parachute Squadron, Royal Engineers, watched Albemarles and Halifaxes towing Horsa gliders carrying some of the British 1st Airborne Division, and Dakotas towing Wacos carrying elements of the American 82nd Airborne Division, pass overhead.

The 1st Air Landing Brigade of the British 1st Airborne Division had been given a difficult target: a bridge, the Ponte Grande near Syracuse. They would land in gliders as near their objective as possible. The 1,200 men were transported in 127 Wacos and 10 Horsas towed by 28 RAF Albemarles and seven Halifaxes, plus 102 Dakotas of the US Troop Carrier Command. American paratroops of the 82nd Division were to drop further west.

Freakish and unforecast weather conditions disrupted the operation. The aircraft had taken off from six airfields and all were buffeted the whole way by an unseasonable storm. A strong headwind scattered tugs and gliders as they approached the island. The Dakota pilots lacked battle experience and adequate training in night flying. Many of them underestimated the wind strength and released their gliders prematurely. Of 137 gliders that were set free, 69 descended onto the storm-wracked sea while 56 were dispersed along Sicily's south-eastern coast. Only 12, all towed by the RAF, landed within their ordained zone. Of a gliderborne force numbering more than 2,000, a mere 100 officers and men were effectively delivered into battle. Only 250 paratroops out of some 3,000 came down in their right dropping zone and the rest were spread over 50 miles (80km). The Horsas, made of wood, stayed afloat for hours and most of those aboard survived. The Wacos, less strongly built and with steel components that, of course, could not float, broke up quickly in the waves. About 300 of the assault force drowned. The anti-aircraft defence also threw some pilots who had never been under fire before into a panic and they rid themselves of the encumbering gliders hastily.

Although so much went awry, this airborne assault played a decisive part in securing the Allied beachhead by delaying the counter-attack of the enemy's reserves.

At the Nuremberg trials after the war, General Student himself declared, "The Allied airborne operation in Sicily was decisive, despite the widely scattered drops which must be expected in a night landing. It is my opinion that if it had not been for the Allied airborne forces blocking the Hermann Goering Armoured Division from reaching the beachhead, that division would have driven the initial seaborne forces back into the sea."

After the landings at Salerno, when the Allies invaded Italy on 3 September 1943, elements of the US 82nd Division took off from Sicilian airfields and parachuted onto the Salerno beachhead.

John Milton, composing "Paradise Lost", visualised a situation in which "With ruin upon ruin, rout on rout/Confusion worse confounded." The invasion of Sicily by air was followed at 2 am by landings from the sea. In the confusion caused by the airborne assault's failure to achieve its objectives the plan was undeniably confounded: in American military jargon it was a Snafu or even a Fubar. Drastic action was imperative to restore the situation. One of the most important targets that had yet to be taken was a massive structure, the Primosole

Below: **Originally planned as a luxurious airliner carrying 36 passengers and four crew, the CW-20 was designed for a twin tail unit with a dihedral tailplane. Production of the civil airliner was not continued but the Curtiss-Wright C-46 was produced as a military freighter. C-46 Commando's saw service in many combat areas of World War Two.** *(JM)*

Bridge. It spanned the Simeto River a mile upstream from its mouth on the Gulf of Catania. The 1st Parachute Squadron, Royal Engineers, was ordered to lead the task.

At 1930hrs on 13 July the paratroops boarded the three USAAF Dakotas that were to take them there. These showed many battle scars, which was reassuring for it meant that their pilots were well experienced. The plan was to go in from the sea at a height of 20ft (6.1m) to avoid Flak, nip over the bridge, then climb steeply to 500ft (152m) over the dropping zone, level off and throttle back for the jump. As they crossed the coast two 88mm shells burst so close to the leading aircraft that its passengers tumbled off their seats. They nearly lost their balance again when the Dakota soared steeply to dropping height. Then came the drop onto a countryside where fires blazed and smoke hung thick, mingling acridly with the stench of high explosive and the dead – men and animals. Next, the Albemarles

arrived, towing Horsas, and the troops they brought debouched amid the familiar noises of battle. It took three days and nights of bloody fighting to wrest the bridge from its stubborn defenders.

This was not the first time the British had used gliders on an offensive operation. That distinction belongs to a raid on Norway on 19 November 1942. At Vemork, deep in the mountains of southern Norway, the Norsk Hydro Electricity Company had built the only factory in the world producing heavy water in commercial quantities. In heavy water the hydrogen atoms are replaced by deuterium, heavy hydrogen, which boils and freezes at higher temperatures than ordinary water and weighs 11 per cent more. Heavy water can be used to make atomic bombs, which Germany, in secrecy, was trying to do.

In January 1940 a senior employee of the German company I. G. Farben, which held a financial interest in Norsk Hydro, visited Vemork to buy its entire

supply of heavy water and to arrange an increase in its production. He did not explain the reason and was not given a decision. The following month a member of the French Secret Service visited Norsk Hydro for the same purpose, but did confide it to the Managing Director. The latter agreed to the supply, said that it would be provided free of cost as a contribution to the defeat of Germany, and told I. G. Farben that it would not be possible to meet their requirement. When the Germans invaded Norway two months later, of course, the plant fell into their hands.

During the next two years information about Germany's purloining of heavy water from Norway and the reason for it reached the British Secret Service. Meanwhile Hitler had decreed that any Allied troops captured on sabotage or Commando missions would be executed.

On the night of 19 November 1942 two Halifaxes, each towing a Horsa with 17 paratroops aboard, took off from Wick in Scotland bound for Vemork to destroy the production plant. There was thick cloud over most of the 400 mile (645km) route and on the way the radio communication between each aeroplane and its glider became unserviceable. One Halifax and Horsa team, flying low below cloud, crashed in the mountains 10 miles (16km) inland. All six of the crew and three soldiers were killed. All the survivors were executed immediately. The other Halifax, flying at 10,000ft (3,050m), failed to find the signal lights set out by the Norwegians who were collaborating with them, so turned back for home. Near the coast the tow line broke and the Horsa fell into the sea. The Germans captured the troops but this time were ordered to torture them and extract all information relevant to the attack before shooting them.

Above: **The Douglas Dragon saw service, initially as a bomber - the B-23 and later as the C-67 transport. The aircraft shown is the UC-67 prototype featuring all-metal construction and retractable undercarriage. It was powered by two 1600 hp Wright Cyclone GR-2600 - A5B 14-cylinder radial engines.** *(JM)*

CHAPTER FOUR

Atlantic Air Bridge

In July 1940 Canada agreed to allow the American-built
aeroplanes to cross her sovereign territory to a Canadian airfield
whence they could be flown to Britain.

The withdrawal of the British Expeditionary
Force from France in June 1940, with its
two RAF elements, the Advanced Air
Striking Force and the Air Component, was
tacit acknowledgement of defeat in the battles
fought during May and June 1940 that ended with
the retreat to Dunkirk and other ports. It left Britain
in danger of losing the war. The Germans were
planning to invade. They sought to land troops at
Dungeness, in Kent, on England's south coast, then
send their tanks thundering north, east and west,
supported by dive bombers, parachute and gliderborne troops and hordes more flown across the
Channel in Ju 52s and gliders. Invasion barges were
being towed from German, Dutch and Belgian
ports to France's Channel coast. RAF Bomber
Command was attacking them day and night. The
British Army had lost a vast amount of weapons,
from rifles to artillery, plus ammunition, vehicles and
other equipment. Everything was against Britain's
survival except morale: courage and the
determination not to be beaten again. This was
reinforced by a loathing of all dictators and of
Nazism in particular.

The most urgent need was for aeroplanes. The
British factories were working all day and all night.
They were just about building enough fighters for
defence against the air raids that were battering the
country. Bomber production had to take second
place. Anyway, it took longer to build a bomber than
a fighter – a matter of size and the number of
engines. Aircraft designed as bombers were also

used for reconnaissance and their variants were on
essential transportation duties. How could
reinforcement aircraft from overseas be brought fast
enough and in the necessary numbers?

The answer lay 3,000 miles (4,830km) away
across the Atlantic. Britain was saved by her friends
in the USA and a Commonwealth partner, Canada.
America was already selling aircraft to the British,
but they came by sea. For each consignment, transit
time from the factory to shipboard was two weeks.
Another ten to fourteen days were needed to cross
an ocean where enemy submarines, mines and
bombers tried to ensure that not all arrived at their
besieged destination. In the month that war was
declared 41 Allied ships had been sunk by U-boats.
In July 1940 Canada agreed to allow the American-
built aeroplanes to cross her sovereign territory to
a Canadian airfield whence they could be flown to
Britain. Thus was established the operation known
as the Atlantic Bridge: the delivery of aircraft by air,
in which an increasing number of civilian and RAF
pilots and crews would participate. Before long,
mixed crews of RAF, Royal Canadian Air Force and
civilians would fly together. Later, pilots of the
United States Army Air Force (USAAF) would join
them. In the month that the air ferry began, U-boats
sank 56 ships.

The RAF could not yet spare any pilots or
wireless operators (known in the USA as radio
operators) who transmitted and received Morse. In
the RAF, the term "radio" was used for voice
transmissions and "wireless" for Morse. (When radar

In the graffiti on the aircraft:

HOLLYWOOD   CAPT. PAPPY. RYAN —

We the 'Men of Gander'
Wish our Hero, Donald well.
When he catches up with Adolph
The 'Fuhrer' will get Hell

fuel OK

BERLIN

Above: **Ready for the long flight from Gander to Britain, Captain 'Pappy' Ryan is handed some last minute documentation before boarding the Lockheed Hudson. Note the well-drawn graffiti on the side of the Hudson.** *(BR)*

was first installed in night fighters in 1940 the men who operated it were called radio operators, to disguise their function. The word "radar" did not even exist in the British vocabulary until the USAAF introduced it in 1942.)

Airlines traversing the American continent were no longer totally dependent on wireless and Morse code as an aid to navigation: radio beacons, to which the pilots themselves listened, took its place. So there was a dearth of wireless operators, who would be needed on the Atlantic crossings as there were no radio beacons at sea. A school to train these "wops" was opened in Montreal. All manner of pilots volunteered to fly the new aircraft, from commercial airline captains to private owners of small pleasure types.

The first machines to be delivered by the new route were Lockheed Hudsons, the military version of the Lockheed 14 Super Electra airliner, with two 1100hp Wright Cyclone engines. The later mark had two Pratt and Whitney Twin Wasp Alvis Leonides. RAF Coastal Command had started to receive the type just before the war for anti-submarine work. Four transport squadrons in the Middle East, four in the Far East and five UK-based meteorological squadrons also flew them in due course. Ultimately just over 2,000 were delivered to the RAF.

Canada's most easterly airfield was at Gander, in Newfoundland. On 10 November 1940 seven Bostons took off for the RAF station at Aldergrove, in Northern Ireland. These were twin engine, powered by the Pratt and Whitney Wasp S3C-G.

Fifteen of this Mark were the first to be delivered, for use as conversion trainers. Mks III to V were light day-bombers with twin 1600hp Wright Cyclone GR-2600-A5B engines. The crews on this first delivery comprised one Australian, six Canadians, six Britons and nine Americans. The pilot of the leading one was Captain Donald Bennett of Imperial Airways, who had previously held a Short Service RAF Commission (four years and four more in the Reserve). The rest of the Bostons followed at short intervals and took up a loose formation astern of him. Frequent wireless messages between them enabled them to check their navigation.

They had an early experience of the weather conditions with which they would have to cope for the next few years: at 20,000ft (6,100km) they met extreme turbulence and a snowstorm that drastically reduced visibility, so Bennett told them to break formation. For another Imperial Airways captain, R.E. Adams, his second pilot and the wireless operator it was an introduction to the kind of problems inherent in flying aircraft across the Atlantic that were virtually straight from the factory. The first alarm was an oil leak. The second was a short circuit in the wireless that could have exploded the ever-present petrol vapour. The third was petrol starvation when one of the tanks ran dry and both engines started to cut. The fourth was when the radio compass became unserviceable. It took over an hour to repair the wireless and resume confident navigation. They landed at RAF Station Aldergrove, in Northern Ireland, five hours later. Two of the

other Hudsons had already landed and within three hours the rest were all down. The seven crews, who had been looking forward to a pleasant break ashore, had to leave the same day by sea on their return journey to Canada.

The transatlantic flights by land aircraft were augmented from January 1941 by Catalina flying boats. The chosen departure point was Bermuda, 600 miles (965km) off the east coast of the USA. The destination was Milford Haven in South Wales. The RAF had ordered one "Cat" before the war, which flew across in July 1939. Thirty more were bought

be sent, the ailerons damaged beyond use. It managed to complete the flight, however, in 10 minutes less than 29 hours.

In addition to the civilians on the transatlantic ferry service, the following month found 24 RAF crews bringing the B-17 Flying Fortress and B-24 Liberator from Montreal to Prestwick, near Ayr on the Scottish west coast. But the turnround was not brisk: all crews, Service and civilian, were returning to Canada by sea, which could take from 10 days to a fortnight; so there were always more aeroplanes awaiting delivery than crews available to fly them. Seven B-24s were therefore provided in which they could go back to Montreal as quickly as possible.

America again showed its concern for the RAF's urgent need. In June 1941 President Roosevelt offered the help of the US Army Air Forces in flying aircraft from factories to Montreal or any other Canadian airfield. (The Service title was changed that month from US Army Air Corps and in March 1942 changed again to US Army Air Force, in the singular.)

In July RAF Ferry Command came into being and four months later quit Montreal for Dorval, a much bigger airfield in the same area built specially for the ferry operation. From the outbreak of war, the majority of pilots and navigators were being trained in the USA and, under the Empire Air Training Scheme, in Canada. (Many were trained also in South Africa and Rhodesia.) Some of these were experienced enough to be entrusted with delivering new aircraft for Ferry Command before being posted to their duties in the UK: they had to have at least 250 flying hours, then underwent special instruction.

The next innovation was a change of route. For twin-engine aircraft, with their considerably less endurance than four-engine types, there was little safety margin when making the crossing. A new airfield that had three runways 2,300 yards (2,100m) long was built at Goose Bay, in the wilds of Labrador. Aeroplanes setting off from Dorval now refuelled

Above: **Before the first Douglas DC-4 airliner had been completed, the US Army took over the production lines. The DC-4 was converted for use as a military transport and cargo carrier. It was designated C-54 by the Army and later named Skymaster. The first C-54 was test flown in April 1942 and large numbers were ordered before the end of that year. The US Government funded the building of a plant exclusively for the production of the C-54.** *(BR)*

and transatlantic delivery flights started in January 1941. Again, there were seven aircraft all setting off by night in the first batch. And once again danger struck one of them. At 20,000ft (6,100km) its automatic pilot jammed and it spun down 19,400ft (5,910km), its aerial breaking before an SOS could

Above: **Lockheed 18 Lodestar served with the US Army as a transport designated C-56, 57, 59, 60 and 66 whilst the US Navy variant was designated R50-1, 2 and 5. The RAF operated the type as Lodestar I and II.** *(JM)*

Above right: **The forerunner to the Hudson this Lockheed Model 14 Super Electra awaits delivery to the US Army as a C-63.** *(JM)*

Right: **A consolidated Liberator C Mk IX in RAF transport service. The single fin model was used in service by the US Navy as the PB4Y patrol bomber and the RY transport.** *(BR)*

there. Two more refuelling stops were arranged, in Greenland and Iceland.

Soon after the ferry service was firmly established, Donald Bennett was recalled to the RAF with the rank of wing commander, commanding a Halifax squadron. By the time the Pathfinder Force was formed in 1942 he was a group captain and, on being appointed to command the new force, was promoted to Air Commodore and eventually Air Vice Marshal.

Among the men who were flying the Atlantic were some of the world's most experienced pilots. One of these was Ernest K. Gann, an American who had qualified for his licence in the early 1920s and became one of the best-known writers of books about flying. He had flown DH4s, which had first taken to the sky as RFC bombers in 1917 and were now carrying mail across America. He had flown airliners and freight carriers on routes that took him to many parts of the world. Even for him, there were daunting moments on the transatlantic ferry route.

The Douglas C-47, known in the RAF as DC-3 Dakota, is probably the best known of all transport aeroplanes. It had first flown as an airliner in 1935 with twin Wasp R-1830-92s. A transport variant for the USAAF was produced in October 1941. Gann made his maiden ferry flight in one. About the eve of departure he wrote, "It was true enough that little fuel was available and the means for transporting and storing the precious stuff had still to be constructed. Radio navigational aids, except in the United Kingdom, were scanty, and those very few operating were far from reliable. Weather analysis and the

forecasting of winds aloft was so random and speculative it was pure folly to trust anything drawn on the charts. There were no facilities for the handling of either men or planes in any numbers. And winter was coming. Into this we flew, not to be plagued by bullets, but always beset by the fiendish technical complications of modern war."

The first leg, from Goose Bay to Greenland, 1,300 miles (2,090km) across the Labrador Sea, was nearly his last flight before he got his angels' wings. The destination was the airfield named Blue-West-One. At briefing, he and his crew were shown a film taken from an aeroplane flying up the west coast of Greenland. There were three fjords, all of which looked identical on the approach. Two ended abruptly in mountainous cliffs. The puzzle was to find the right triplet. Blue-West-One lay 60 miles (96km) up it, under the ice cap, and would not come in sight until the last bend was rounded. Oh, yes – and the single runway was not level: aircraft landed uphill and took off down. On an island lying off the entrances to these there was a radio range transmitter; like almost everything to do with flying this route, it was unreliable. The film showed a ship that had run ashore half-way up the fjord they would be seeking – a rather depressing way of

checking their position. If they found themselves in the wrong fjord, there was no room to about turn. There was no alternative airfield. If the fog and low cloud that usually hampered navigation and visual identification at this season befell them, they had no choice but to return to base before venturing into any fjord. If they did turn back, they would probably run out of fuel before they could make it back to Goose Bay.

The aircraft had done a lot of hours and wallowed like a sow in a quagmire. Gann and Johnson, his co-pilot, had to fly hands–on every inch of the way. With no exterior aids by which to navigate, they had to

rely on star sights with the octant. Eventually Greenland came into view but they did not appear to be getting any closer. They concluded that they must have been flying into a headwind. They managed to take a bearing on the radio range. There was stratus cloud all the way to the coastline. They entered it and without knowing what the altimeter setting should be, began groping their way at what they hoped was a safe altitude: the mountains' height was not known; there were tall icebergs; and it was misty. The film they had seen showed the fjords with clarity and was obviously taken on a clear, sunny day, which made identifying the right one

Above: **Lockheeds model 49 Constellation first flown on 9 January 1943 was immediately taken over by the military and designated C-69.** *(BR)*

Above right: **Consolidated C-87 Liberator Express** was generally similar to the B-24 Liberator bomber , but without gun turrets. The bomb bay area has been modified and equipped as a passenger cabin; note the side windows. *(JM)*

Above: **Boeing Model 314A** flying boat was a civil aircraft used for the transport of military personnel. The aircraft G-AGCA was operated by British Overseas Airways and named Berwick. *(BR)*

Left: **Douglas C-54 Skymaster** being loaded at Gander, Newfoundland prior to the Atlantic crossing. *(JM)*

Above: **Caproni Ca 133's of No 61 Squadron of the Italian Air Force during the Ethiopia campaign prior to World War Two. Although deployed originally as a bomber these aircraft, powered by three 450 hp Piaggio P.VIII RC14 Stella seven-cylinder radial engines, gave sterling service as transports and ambulances in Libya and the Russian Front until 1943.** *(HC)*

Right: **A Caproni Ca 133 Sanatario (ambulance) being prepared for operations.** *(HC)*

appear much easier than this. But they spotted the wrecked ship and a little while later landed.

They had brought a cargo of steel girders. These were replaced next morning by a load of lavatory paper. The navigator muttered, "Just what the hell am I going to say when they ask me what I did in the war?"

But there was also an engine for a P-38 fighter and there were brooms, filing cabinets, metal wastepaper baskets, and fragmentation bombs whose weight was unknown, and were therefore held responsible for the DC-3's sluggish rate of climb.

On take-off, they made climbing turns until they broke cloud. Then they entered thick overcast cloud and had to fly on instruments. They did not know how high the ice cap was, but would find out when they crossed it on their way to Iceland – or if they crashed into it. They had been told that they would need a minimum of 9,000ft (2,745m) to clear it. This was useful knowledge, but not exactly encouraging: if they lost an engine, they would not be able to make better than 6,000ft (1,830m) until they had used a lot of petrol. They had also been warned that they might see U-boats on this leg. The helpful instructions they had been given were that they must record the sighting but avoid being seen themselves. And, in further encouragement, when they neared Iceland they could perhaps encounter enemy aircraft, Focke-Wulf Condors that had a range of 2,206 miles (3,549km) and bristled with weaponry.

They left Greenland behind, and the hours passed with no radio contact with Iceland. They reduced altitude to 3,000ft (915m), night fell and they were in cloud. Navigating by dead reckoning gave no accurate assurance of their position: all that Gann could reason was that their destination just had to be close. They descended. At 1,000ft (305m) they had not yet broken through cloud. At 500ft (150m) the visibility was no better. At 300ft (91m) some unorthodox means of finding the island had to be the only resort.

At the end of the radio aerial, a wire wound

Above: **Powered by three 750 hp Alfa Romeo 126 RC-34 nine cylinder radial engines, the Savoia Marchetti SM.83 was first used by civil airlines before being requisitioned by the Italian Air Force and used as a transport in World War Two. Shown is the prototype first flown in 1937.** *(BR)*

Right: **Savoia Marchetti SM-95 of the Italian Air Force. This clean looking four-engined transport was only built in small numbers.** *(HC)*

Below: **The Caproni Ca 309 was originally developed as a twin-engined bomber. Later it was also used as a transport including the Ca 309s (Sanatario) ambulance version.** *(HC)*

Below: **First flown on 14 October 1940, the Fiat G-12 was an all-metal design, featuring a retractable undercarriage, was capable of carrying 22 fully-equipped soldiers. An extra long-range version, the G-12TA-GR, was built for the purpose of maintaining air liaison with Japan. Production of the G-12 was re-started in 1947. (HC)**

round a reel under the DC-3's belly, was a lead weight. Streamed astern in the slipstream this weight was about 50ft (15m) above whatever surface was beneath them – land or sea. Gann told the radio operator to open the small hatch that gave access to the reel and aerial, and hold the wire. The co-pilot was doing the flying. He was told to continue descending and as soon as the radio man felt the lump of lead hit either water or solid earth, he was to shout and the pilot would level off. And that was how they found their way to the airfield on a cloudy night.

Coolness under fire is the severest test of a soldier, sailor or airman. For airmen there are other equally unnerving ordeals and tests of courage. Men like Ernest Gann and his crew experienced them often and passed with what one can aptly describe as flying colours. Their only reward was self-respect and the esteem of their comrades. Civilians have no medals to mark their bravery.

Italy's Air Transport Operation

In the early 1930s the attention of the Italian Air Force turned to the building of bomber/transport aircraft. The first was the Caproni Ca.101, comparable to the RAF Wapiti and Vincent general purpose types. It had three 235hp Alfa Romeo engines and made its first flight in 1932. The Ca.111, with a single 950hp Isotta-Fraschini, first flew in 1933. The 133, flew in 1935, powered by three 450/460 Piaggio engines and, when the Second World War started, was Italy's main military transport aircraft.

The Savoia-Marchetti SM81 transport aeroplane, which had been in service since 1935, was a variant of a civil airliner. A trimotor type, it had been powered by a variety of engines: 700hp Piaggio PX, 580hp Alfa Romeo 125, 680hp Piaggio P IX, 900hp Alfa Romeo 126, 1,000hp Gnome-Rhne. Its

Far left: **Damaged on a desert airfield aSavoia Marchetti SM.82 was of that company's many trimotor designs. Used originally as a civil airliner all were later requisitioned by the Italian Air Force in 1939.** *(BR)*

Left: **Piaggio's P-108 was built in two versions; P-108B a bomber and the P-108C, shown here, a transport. In 1947, Paiggo began production of the P-108T-2 (a modernised version of the wartime aircraft) for civil airlines.** *(BR)*

wingspan was 78ft 9in (24m), length 58ft 5in (17.81m), height 14ft 7in (4.44m). The empty weight was 13,890lb (6,300kg), loaded weight 23,040lb (10,450kg), maximum speed 211mph (339km/h), range 932 miles (1,500km).

The SM82, first delivered to the Italian Air Force in 1939, had three 950hp Alfa Romeo 128RC21 engines. Wingspan was 96ft 10in (29.51m), length 73ft 10in (22.50m), height 18ft (5.49m), empty weight 26,455lb (12,000kg), loaded weight 39,728lb (18,020kg). It had seats for 40 troops and could carry a cargo of 13,273lb (6,020kg). Maximum speed 204mph (325km/h), range 2,467 miles (3,970km). It was armed with one or two 12.7mm or from two to five 7.7mm machine guns.

None of these aircraft was designed solely to transport troops or materiel. All were meant also for bombing, ground strafing, reconnaissance, troop-carrying and supplying forward positions, and were capable of short take-off and landing. The reason for all these characteristics was that Italy, which had had a colony in Eritrea, north-east Africa, since 1885 and, like Britain and France, had colonised part of Somaliland (Somalia), intended to seize more territory in neighbouring Abyssinia (Ethiopia) and anywhere else in the area that was defended by men in loincloths carrying spears. Machine gunning and bombing people who could not shoot back was a safe way to fight; and where there was a lack of airfields, STOL capability was important.

When Italy entered the war, 10 months after Germany, 14 squadrons were flying the Ca.133. It could carry either 2,200lb (998kg) of bombs, or troops or freight to the same weight. Its top speed was only 174mph (280km/h) and range 839 miles (1,350km). It was armed with either two 7.7mm or one 12.7mm dorsal machine guns, one 7.7mm fired through a belly hatch and two beam 7.7s.

The following information comes from a recent Italian Air Ministry statement: "The Air Force developed air transport only during the Second World War". It goes on to say: "When, on 4th June 1940 the Air Force carried out the transformation of civil aviation for the war, creating the Special Air Services (SAS) and its relative command (CSAS), and decided to assign also to these, apart from civil aircraft in service, the S82, originally conceived as a long-range bomber, the development and importance that this structure, created by modest means and with a programme of limited occasional use, would assume was not foreseen.

"Initially, the transport units were provided with the S81, S82 and G12 (military version of Cant seaplane, Gabbiano), not suitably built or equipped for transporting a variety of freight. The construction of S82 and G12 transport variants was intensified. The number of transport squadrons was greatly increased and the arm was given autonomy. (In December 1942, it had 700 pilots.)"

Left: **Savoia Marchetti's SM.84 was designed as a fast bomber but was used mainly in the communications and transport role. It differed from other SM designs by having a twin-fin tailplane assembly. The SM.84 shown is in Luftwaffe markings.** *(HC)*

Left: **The Savoia Marchetti SM.82 was first delivered to the Italian Air Force in 1939. Powered by three 950hp Alfa Romeo 128R-C21 radial engines it could carry 40 troops or 13273 lbs (6020 kg) of cargo.** *(HC)*

The following SAS statistics apply to the period 10 June 1940 to 31 December 1942:

Sorties	38,428
Flying hours	151,431
Passengers carried	504,146
Tons of freight carried	34,190
Aircraft lost	121
Crew members lost	196

The statistics below are for the Air Force.

Sorties	38,428
Flying hours	19,288
Passengers carried	27,580
Tons of freight carried	2,734
Aircraft lost	2
Crew members lost	4

"The figures for SAS operations 1st January to 10th May 1943 in Tunisia, rounding up the figures, and the total including operations in other zones (Greece, the Aegean, Albania, Slovenia, Sardinia, Sicily, etc), the approximate totals are:"

Sorties	44,000
Passengers carried	580,000
Tons of freight carried	40,000
No of aircraft lost	210
Crew members lost	430

tives. The Russians were not passive defenders; they took the battle to the invader. Between early February and mid-May the Germans evacuated 25,400 casualties by air. They were also delivering supplies to the tune of 64,884 tonnes, and reinforcements – 30,500 of them. To transport men and materiel by aeroplane and glider involved 32,427 and 659 sorties respectively. The price paid was the loss of 265 aircraft.

In late November 1942 Germany again undertook a relief operation on a grand scale. The minimum requirement was to transport a daily 700 tonnes, which would need 500 sorties by Ju 52s and Ju 86s. On Day One, 300 tonnes were flown in on 320 sorties. Adverse weather limited delivery over the next two days to a total of 130 tonnes. Three days later 100 tonnes were lifted and 190 He 111s were added to the cargo fleet. At the end of the third week in December the record of 700 tonnes were delivered in 450 sorties. Then Russian tanks appeared and 60 aircraft were destroyed while 108 Ju 52s and 16 Ju 86s were withdrawn. Eventually, only drops were feasible and on 2 February 1943 the German Armies in Russia surrendered.

A typical show of Polish bravery occurred in July 1944, when the proximity of Russian forces prompted the Resistance organisation in Warsaw to take up arms against them in the expectation of strong support from outside. By 6 August they

Above: **Four factory-new Junkers JU552/3m awaiting delivery from Junkers Dessau works. Two are in Legion Kondor markings ready for service, crewed by members of the Luftwaffe, in Spain.** *(HC)*

Right: **German troops pouring out of the nose doors of a Messrschmitt Me 323D-1. This enormous aircraft began life as a glider but later this powered version was designed and put into production in early 1942.** *(HC)*

Right: **A Junkers JU52/3m in Luftwaffe markings. Powered by (wartime versions) three 830hp BMW 132T nine-cylinder radial engines this robustly constructed aircraft had good STOL performance due to highly efficient Junker's patented 'double wing' flaps. The JU52/3m continued in production after the war in France as the AAC.1 and in Spain as the CASA 352L. The final aircraft being built in 1952 to be withdrawn from service in 1975.** *(BR)*

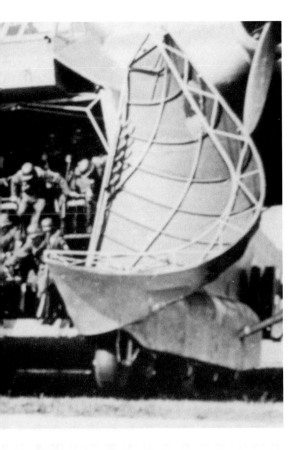

controlled the city. RAF transport and bomber aircraft flown by British, Polish and South African crews flew 93 sorties between 12 and 17 August, but suffered 17 losses. This scale was too costly to sustain. Polish squadrons made a few more deliveries and the USAAF sent 107 bombers to do a high-altitude drop, but only 19 out of 1,200 containers fell into the Resistance members' hands. On 16 September the insurrection was crushed.

World War Two

In 1939 Germany's air transport force was the best equipped in the world, but no new types of aircraft had been added to it. Throughout the war the Ju 52 was Germany's most numerous transport aircraft. It needed a 1,640ft (500m) landing strip, which was a handicap. Two manufacturers, Arado and Henschel, competed to produce a successor to it and the former was successful with the Ar 232. This made its first flight in April 1941 and the prototype was delivered in May 1942. Its innovative features were a high wing, which gave unobstructed access to the cargo hold, a high tail boom with full-width rear doors below it, a level floor at truck height, short take-off and landing capability and a multi-wheel landing gear. This last consisted of 22 close-set small wheels that enabled it to cross ditches and trenches and earned it the name of "Centipede" (Tausendfüssler). The A series had twin 1,600hp BMW 801MA engines and the B series four 1,200hp BMW Bramo 323R-2. Only five were delivered for service.

Another newcomer was the Ju 290, which was first used at Stalingrad and had been derived from the Ju 90 airliner, which in turn was a derivative of the Ju 89 bomber. It had four BMW 801D 1,700hp or 801E 1970hp. Wingspan was 137ft 9.5in (42m), length 29ft 1in (8.86m), height 22ft 5in (6.83m).

The Russian campaign eventually saw the German forces *in extremis* and Heinkel 111 bombers were often used as transports. One flying boat type figured in the Luftwaffe's inventory, the Blohm und Voss BV 222. This was described as a strategic transport. The prototype was the first of three ordered by the national airline, Lufthansa, who ultimately did not receive it. Instead, after its first flight, on 7 September 1940, it was modified as a freight transport. Nine more followed, each of them different from all its predecessors, and a final four. All were six-engined: the first six were petrol, the next six diesel, after which the manufacturer reverted to petrol. The Luftwaffe received 13, which shuttled between northern Norway and North Africa with urgent stores. All but four were shot down or destroyed at their moorings. The leading particulars of all were: six 1,000hp BMW Bramo

Right: **The Messerschmitt Me323 Gigant (Giant) was constructed mainly from welded steel tube covered with plywood and fabric. Power to lift this giant was supplied by six 1140 hp Gnome-Rhone 14N 48/49 14-cylinder two row radial engines allowing a top speed of 177 mph and a range of 684 miles. The Me 323 was a very vulnerable air transport, 14 being shot down by Beaufighters, of the RAF, whilst airlifting petrol to Rommel's beleaguered Afrika Korps.** *(HC)*

(BMW) Fafnir 323R engines or 980hp Jumo 207C diesels. Wingspan was 150ft 11in (46m), length 121ft 4.½in (37m), height 35ft 9in (10.9m).

Germany, urgently in need of transport aircraft capable of carrying more passengers or cargo than the Ju 52, had built the Me 321 heavy cargo glider that the Luftwaffe first received in 1941, and Me 323 heavy cargo transport aeroplane. Named Gigant (Gigantic), both were a typically Germanic concept, as ill-proportioned and menacing as Berlin's Reichstag or Brandenburger Tor. Both aircraft had the same dimensions.

The 323 production variants had six 1140 Gnome-Rhne 14N 48/49 engines. The most numerous version in the whole range, glider or powered, was the Me 323D-1. All marks had the same dimensions: wingspan 180ft 5in (55m), length 92ft 4.¼in (28.15m), height 33ft 3½in (10.15m), empty weight 321B-1 27,432lb (12,400kg), 323D-6 60,280lb (27,330kg), 323E-1 61,700lb (28,001kg), maximum loaded weight 321 B-1 75,852lb (34,400kg), 323D-6 94,815lb (43,000kg), 323E-1 99,208lb (45,000kg). The maximum speeds were: 321 on tow 160km/h (99mph), 323D 328km/h (204mph).

Getting either 321 or 323 airborne was a Herculean and ridiculous performance. It had to be hauled off the ground – the 323 (with its engines at full bore) by either three Me Bf110s or a specially built Heinkel 111.

When the Axis forces in North Africa were at their last gasp, in the spring of 1943, and desperately in need of every kind of supplies, they increased the number of daytime sorties flown by their transport aircraft. It was not a wise decision. On 10/11 April British and American fighters shot down 24 Ju 52s, many of which were carrying petrol and exploded spectacularly, and 14 escorting Me 109s. On 18 April RAF Spitfires and USAAF Warhawks intercepted about 100 Ju 52s, which they shot down for the loss of seven Allied fighters. On 22 April Me 323s loaded with petrol were attacked by 90 Spitfires and Kittyhawks that wiped them all out. Between 5 and 22 April the RAF, South African Air Force and USAAF destroyed 433 Ju 52s and Me 323s. Among the attacking fighters were the most versatile of all – Beaufighters, armed with six machine guns and four cannons.

Designed as night fighters, they were also in action with torpedoes and rockets against shipping, with rockets and cannon against ground targets, and with machine guns and cannon as day fighters. In what the Americans call a turkey shoot, when the Beaus committed mayhem among the Me 323s that day they shot down 14.

One of the least known uses of the Ju 52 was to carry troops to Baghdad. In 1930 Iraq began to

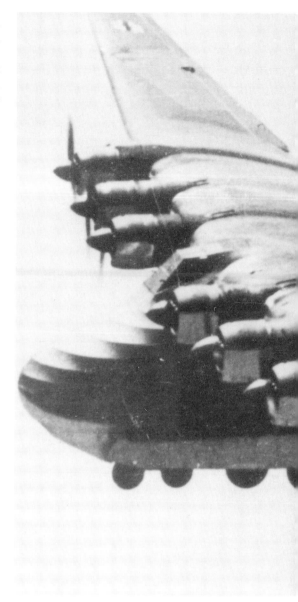

govern itself with a continued British diplomatic and military presence. The RAF had a flying school at Habbaniya, 43 miles (70km) west of Baghdad. Rashid Ali, the Prime Minister, was an enemy of the British and actively pro-German. The King, Feisal II, was 11 years old and an uncle was regent. On 1 April 1941 Rashid Ali and a group of Army officers seized power. The regent fled to Transjordan next day.

Valentias and Dakotas, the latter borrowed from two airlines but flown by RAF pilots, brought reinforcements to Basra. From there, some went by air to the RAF station at Shaiba; the rest, 343 officers and men of the King's Own Royal Rifles, to Habbaniya. Rashid Ali asked Germany for military help. Me 110s and He 111 bombers were sent with Ju 52s carrying troops. Their route was Athens to Rhodes – Aleppo to Damascus – Mosul – Baghdad. On 2 May Iraqi

Far right: **Loading a Maybach gun tractor towing a 88mm Flak gun in through the nose doors of a Me 323D-1.** *(HC)*

troops opened fire on the airfield. The RAF and Army put up a valiant defence; training aircraft attacked the enemy with bombs in improvised racks. The Germans bombed and machine gunned. A British relief column arrived, but by then the Germans had withdrawn from the battle and flown away. There was a minor troop-carrying operation during the fighting in Sicily, when German paratroops were dropped between Syracuse and Lenten.

The last German parachute drop of the Second World War was made on 17 December 1944 at Hoe Venn, which, at 2,283ft (696m), was the highest part of the Ardennes. It was not a finale for the 450 paratroops who jumped from 67 Ju 52s to savour in retrospection. The weather was bad and made navigation difficult.

There were many injuries and only a few men reached the target. Nonetheless, Oberstleutnant von den Heydte and those of his soldiers who were unhurt and dropped at the right place held out for three days. For them there was much to give pride and pleasure when reminiscing.

During the Germans' withdrawal from the Balkans, a lengthy operation that began in October 1944 and did not finish until February 1945, Ju 52s landed supplies at places along the withdrawal route.

Ju 232s and FW Condors based at Vienna supplied the Germans occupying Crete. They had to fly by night to avoid being shot down by the RAF. This operation ceased on 8 May 1945.

The Pacific and Far East

The Japanese began training paratroops at four schools, two each for the Army and Navy, in early 1940. Their equipment was poor, casualties were frequent and the output was slow: each course took six months. That summer Germany sent four instructors to Japan; they brought better equipment and shortened the courses to two months of intensive training. Fifteen months later the number of German instructors had increased to 100, there were nine training schools, and 14,000 soldiers and sailors were under instruction. The naval system at first offered little prospect of survival: either the inadequate four-week training or the enemy would do for the bulk of them. The course was accordingly lengthened in the autumn. A unique feature of all the training was jumps at 350ft (106m), which caused heavy loss of life from 'chutes failing to open.

Air landing units were planned but no gliders were built in Japan until 1944. Used on only one operation – to lift reinforcements on to Luzon in 1945.

The paratroopers' maiden assault was against Menado airfield in the Celebes immediately after a bomber raid and strafing by fighters. The Dutch defenders fought gallantly and few survived, the locally enlisted troops resisted briefly before decamping. On 14 January the oil refineries and airfield at Palembang in Sumatra were the objectives. The airfield was bombed first, but there

Far left **The Junkers Ju-290 prototype for the Ju-290 VI military transport was developed from the civilian Junkers Ju-90 airliner, which in turn was a derivative of the Ju-89 bomber.** *(HC)*

Far left below: **A production Ju-290 VI awaiting flight test at Junkers factory at Dessau.** *(HC)*

Below: **Designed originally for Deutsche Luft Hanse in 1937 the Focke-Wulf FW200 Condor soon found a place in the newly formed Luftwaffe as a maritime reconnaissance bomber. Many were used as transports.** *(BR)*

Right: **The Junkers
Ju-252 VI was an
all-metal
trimotor. Later in
the war Junkers
produced the
Ju-352 but this
was built mainly
of wood
although in looks
it was almost
identical. The
Ju-252 shown is
camouflaged but
carries a civilian
registration
D-ADCC.** (HC)

Below: **Designed
originally as a
regional airliner,
the Blohm und
Voss BV 144
featured a
variable
incidence wing
and other high-
lift devices.
Development
was slow, the
first prototype
was assembled
and flown at the
Brequet factory,
Bayonne, France,
in August 1994.
The project was
abandoned soon
after the
liberation of
France.** (HC)

were no fighters within range to ground strafe. Two waves of 35 aircraft each dropped 300 troops, of whom 200 were killed along with 16 aeroplanes shot down. On 21 February, after strafing fighters had attacked, 350 paras were dropped on Timor and this was followed by a landing from the sea.

There was no further paratroop or gliderborne assault in the Pacific for nearly a year. On 29 January 1943, Port Moresby in New Guinea,

under attack by the Japanese, was reinforced by 57 USAAF Dakotas with two Australian infantry battalions aboard. Further infantry and artillery were lifted in during the next two days. Faced with this increased Allied strength, the Japanese fell back. It was the beginning of the retreat that would end when the atom bombs were dropped. In China, the Chinese Nationalist Army came under attack by 60 Japanese troops once, in 1943.

A remarkable Allied parachute operation in

Above: **A Douglas C-54D Skymaster of the Twentieth Troop Carrier Squadron USAF is loaded with coal in preparation for a delivery flight to Berlin.** *(HC)*

Left: **Curtiss-C-46 Commando, the US forces most powerful twin-engined troop/freight carrier.** *(JM)*

Right: **Douglas C-47 Skytrain, workhorse of the Allied forces, being prepared ready to load supplies for a forward nbase. Photographed in the Pacific theatre at the latter part of World War Two, the aircraft in the background is a Boeing B-17 Flying Fortress.** *(HG)*

Below: **On a pre-acceptance test flight this new Douglas C 47 Skytrain, flys along the Californian coast near to the Douglas Burbank plant.** *(HG)*

315972

Below: **A posed photograph of troops loading a Douglas C-68. Note the prewar US Army insignia.** *(HG)*

Right: **Designated C-64 by the USAF the Noorduyn Norseman was used as a light personnel transport and freighter. In this posed photograph, blood plasma is being unloaded prior to delivery to a military hospital.** *(JM)*

Left: **Last in the series of Lockheed's fast twin-engined transports was the model 18 Lodestar. It was first flown in 1939 was used in many record attempts, a Loadstar broke the American Transcontinental Record in November 1940. The Lockheed Ventura, for the RAF (USAF B-34) and the PV-1 Harpoon for the US Navy were both direct developments.** *(Lockheed)*

Below: **Another view of a C-64 Norseman, it was in an aircraft of this type that disappeared over the English Channel whilst carrying bandleader Glenn Miller.** *(JM)*

Above: **Douglas C-54 Skymasters being refuelled at Gander, Newfoundland, Canada prior to the flight across the Atlantic to Prestwick, Scotland.** *(JM)*

Right: **Loading a C-46 Commando, these aircraft were also used on the North Atlantic supply route.** *(JM)*

Left: **A Douglas C-54 Skymaster on a pre-delivery test flight.** *(HG)*

Above: **Fairchilds C-82 Packets did not see service in World War Two, only three had been built by VJ-Day.** *(JM)*

Right: **The US Presidential transport in 1949 was a Douglas VC-118 (DC-6), replacing an earlier C-54 also named 'The Independence'.** *(HG)*

Right: **Avro Ansons first entered RAF service in 1936 and served in a variety of roles in World War Two. Since 1945 it was used only as a trainer or communications aircraft.** *(JM)*

Above: **Douglas Super DC-3 operated by the US Navy as the R4D-8.** (BR)

Left: **A Douglas R5D-1 of the Naval Air Transport Service over San Francisco Bay.** (HG)

Left: **US Navy postwar colour scheme on a Douglas R5D-1.** (HG)

Top: **Junkers Ju90's were used prewar by Lufthansa, but in 1940 the entire fleet was requisitioned by the Luftwaffe.** *(HC)*

Top right: **The Arado Ar.232, a four-engined transport, featured a unique multi-wheeled undercarriage.** *(HC)*

May 1944 broke some of the established precepts for this type of assault, under the pressure of extreme urgency. A large-scale counter-attack was to be launched in New Guinea. The flat land in the valley of the Markham river was the main objective, one of the rare places where several airstrips could be laid quickly. The American 503rd Parachute Infantry Regiment, which had not jumped since the North African landings in November 1942, was flown to Australia, where the 2/4 Field Regiment (artillery) joined them. The gunners were given two days' hasty instruction, during which they each made only one drop. Dakotas could not accommodate 25-pounder guns, which therefore had to be carried under the aircraft's bellies. The means of doing this had to be extemporised by the artillerymen. Bombers,

freighters and 96 Dakotas comprised a total of 292 aeroplanes, of which 96 lifted 1,700 paratroops. The mission was handsomely accomplished.

Ten months later a poorly planned drop was made by the US 503rd on Kamiri airfield near Noemfoor, New Guinea. The initial assault was amphibious and successful. It is hard to understand why air assaults were called for at all, let alone ones that had not been rehearsed in the difficulties entailed in dropping troops on a long, narrow airstrip. The pilots, who had never before dropped parachutists, came in too fast and too low – some at an imbecilic 200ft (60m). To aggravate this ineptitude, a strong wind was blowing. The paras were widely scattered and suffered many casualties. Some were dragged along the ground; some descended on tall trees from which they fell

and were injured; some slammed onto the runway itself; and others onto a variety of the usual obstacles that were strewn about military airfields, such as accumulator trolleys, vehicles and gun posts. Notwithstanding this discouraging experience, a second lift was made next day, with the same ugly consequences. The men who were not injured then fought alongside infantry and gunners in clearing the enemy out. The fourth landing was again amphibious.

The last American paratroop drops were made on 16 February 1945 at Corregidor, a small island of rock off Manila Bay where 6,000 Japanese troops were stationed. The only flat surfaces not covered by defensive artillery, machine guns and riflemen, were each 250 yards (228m) long and

150 yards (137m) wide. Both were atop 400ft (122m) cliffs that fell sheer to the sea. The aircraft were again C-47s, 51 of them this time. Fifty of them, carrying a battalion, had each to make three runs because the dropping zone was so small. One circled overhead, controlling the attack. The first drops began at 0830hrs, followed by a second delivery at noon and a third the following morning. The Japanese were taken by surprise. After 10 days' fighting, during which the US 53rd had 850 casualties, only 27 Japanese survived to be taken prisoner.

In June 1945, the last air landing assault by Allied Troops in World War Two was carried out by the 11th Airborne Division when 1,010 airlifted troops landed at Aparri in seven gliders.

Above: **The Nakajima AT-2 was built originally as a civil airliner, but far greater numbers were produced for the Japanese Army (Ki-34) and their Navy (L1N-1).** *(BR)*

CHAPTER SIX

Burma & India

Flying over the Hump and the mountains of
the India/Burma Frontier.

Since 1931 the Japanese had been striving to annexe as large an area of China as possible. They began by invading the province of Manchuria and making it a satellite state of what was intended to become the Japanese Empire. China's defence was weak. Warlords with their own armies were incessantly fighting one another; and industrially she was primitive, whereas Japan was in many ways as advanced as the West. In 1940 the Japanese established a puppet government in Nanking. In 1941 their forces entered Indo-China. The obvious purpose was to use that country as a base from which to attack Malaya and the East Indies. President Roosevelt of the USA told them to get out. They refused, so the US and British Governments and the Dutch Government in exile in London froze all Japan's assets, which cut it off from its oil supplies.

A Chinese General, Chiang Kai Shek, had by this time formed the Chinese Nationalist Army that nominally represented the whole nation. On 21 January 1942, America having newly entered the war on Britain's side, Roosevelt sent General Joseph Stilwell to China as Chiang Kai Shek's Chief of Staff. Unfortunately Vinegar Joe, as he was known on account of his sour disposition, was a misanthrope who constantly derided, denigrated and obstructed the British armed Services.

The Chinese Nationalist Army had to be supplied with the necessities for making war. This could be done only by air, since the Japanese had cut the Burma Road into China. The USAF and many of the American crews who had flown on the Atlantic ferry made the deliveries. Ernest K. Gann was one of them. Flying back and forth over the mountains between India and China was no more a sinecure than on the India-Burma route. Everest and K3 stood at the north of this stretch of the Himalayas and the wind from Tibet tore down upon the mountains that separated Assam from China.

On his first trip Gann flew as co-pilot to a Major Sweeney. As he pointed out, his situation was anomalous. He was a civilian with an identity card which "identified me, however ridiculously, as a noncombatant. The Japanese were holding much of the area over which we would fly and their fighters did what they could to harass the operation". He had been made to wear a gun belt with a holstered Service pistol, which he did not want, lent to him by a colleague. "If we met with any of the misfortunes" that had been described to him "wouldn't it be rather embarrassing to explain my status and the gun?" He could, almost certainly would, be shot as a *franc tireur*. He was immediately given a major's rank insignia, a gold oak leaf, to wear on his collar lapels. The departure airfield was in Assam. There was a variety of aeroplanes there, many of them unserviceable for lack of spare parts. The C-47s were not suited to their task. Their two engines could not drag them high enough to cross the Hump with a full load. They often had to weave through the tortuous passes "and too many

young Air Force pilots were killed in the doing".

Some North-West Airline pilots were ferrying Curtiss C–46s from the States to Assam. These performed better than the Douglas C-47s because they had more powerful engines, two 2,000hp Pratt & Whitney R-2800-51 Double Wasp, and later two 2,200hp R-2800-75. Wingspan was 108ft 1in (32.9m), length 76ft 4in (23.2m), height 21ft 9in (6.6m). Cruising speed was 227mph (365km/h), max range 1,600 miles (2,575km).

C-87s, a B-24 Liberator variant, were also employed. In April 1944 B-29 Superfortress bombers were added to the offensive air strength and some of these were converted to carry fuel supplies for China.

The Flying Tigers

There was another reason for flying the Hump route. It concerns the most bizarre military air force ever formed and, but for the fact that every facet of it has been verified, it would defy credulity. General Chiang Kai Shek's wife had been educated in America and was as strong-willed and dedicated as he. China had a ragtime air force that was a liability in every way. Italy had insinuated its way into China by arranging to train the air force and sell aeroplanes to it. A factory in Nanking assembled the Fiat CR32 fighters that were exported CKD – complete, knocked down – i.e. in parts. Altogether 150 were built, a cosily profitable transaction for

the supplier. No bombers were yet contemplated.

An Italian, General Saroni, was in charge of production and training. The pilots in this farcical unit were mercenaries, mostly American and virtually without exception the drunken, barely competent sweepings of the metaphorical gutters of the aviation world. They were so lacking in aptitude that fatal accidents were abundant; and the machines were highly combustible. Any trainee who completed the course alive was awarded his wings, whatever his ability. Madame Kai Shek induced Lee Chenault, a rock-tough retired 47-year-old Major of the US Army Air Corps (as it was then titled), to accept the job of organising and training this unsavoury outfit. The agreement was for three months and highly paid.

Chennault was still in office a year later, by when most of China was in thrall to the Japanese; who had cut off communication by the Yangtze-Kiang and Yellow rivers and access to the rice crops that fed the population. The Japanese Air Force was present in strength. Chennault had no pilots left, because all the aircraft had been written off in accidents. Persevering with the intention of some day, somehow putting together an effective air force, he stockpiled petrol, ammunition and bombs and studied the Japanese Air Force as it strafed and bombed the Chinese National Army.

Early in 1941 the American Government realised the need to ensure that China remained active against the invaders. Chennault was permitted to form a force to be called the American Volunteer

Above: **The Douglas C-47 Skytrain was the most used air transport aircraft of World War Two. The example shown is in Royal Air Force service, where it was called the Dakota.** *(JM)*

Group (AVG) and fortified with 100 Curtiss P-40 Warhawks. These dated back to 1937, when it was decided to fit them with 1,040hp water-cooled Allison V-1710-33 engines. The wingspan was 37ft 3.½in (11.3m), length 31ft 8½in (9.7m), height 12ft 4in (3.75m). Max speed 345mph (555km/h), range 730 miles (1,175km). This variant was not passed fit for operations but was good enough for Chennault's purpose.

He was also allowed to visit Army Air Corps, Marine and Navy air stations to recruit air and ground crew. His proposition was well received. The AVG would be similar to a squadron in any conventional air force, but less strict and better paid, with a bonus for each enemy aircraft shot down. Their appointment, purpose and presence in China would breach the Geneva Convention, so they were allotted bogus civilian occupations to be recorded in the passports. By nature, the breed of men who would be attracted by this sort of venture were difficult to control, hard drinking, pugnacious and a peril to respectable women. In those ways they were as disreputable as their predecessors of the so-called Chinese Air Force. The Chinese called them tigers and from this the First American Volunteer Group became known as The Flying Tigers. They immediately displayed the skill they had acquired in the various armed Services by being credited with 299 confirmed enemy aircraft destroyed and a possible 600 in six months.

On 3 July 1942 the USA announced its active presence in China. The Flying Tigers were invited to return to their former Services: Chennault to be a Brigadier General and the rest majors or captains. They refused, but were compelled to rejoin. Chennault became commander of the newly named China Air Task Force, but only five of his officers stayed with him. The reconstituted force trained new members and continued fighting the Japanese. They were defiant of Service regulations and an inspecting officer reported that air and ground crew alike were unshaven, wore muddy shoes and shabby uniforms and flouted discipline. They did, however, do their jobs magnificently.

Their presence in China was the primary reason for the Hump operation.

Allied air operations over Burma are recalled mostly as flights across a mountain range whose highest peak rises to 18,833ft (5,740m) in the Naga Hills on the frontier between Burma and the Indian province of Assam. The air crews who had to fly over this formidable barrier and sought to find their way across it through the passes or over lower crests at 10,000ft (3,050m) gave it the wryly understated name of the "Hump".

Burma became another battle front because Japan had entered the war as Germany's ally. On 7 December 1941, at 0755hrs, 40 Japanese torpedo bombers, 50 high-level bombers and 51 dive

bombers, escorted by 40 fighters, had flown off six aircraft carriers to make a surprise attack on the United States Navy's base at Pearl Harbour, Hawaii – before Japan had declared war. A second wave of similar strength, with the torpedo aeroplanes replaced by more dive bombers, attacked immediately after. For the loss of 29 aircraft, the Japanese had destroyed 188 and damaged all eight of the American battleships in port, of which five were sinking. Three cruisers and three destroyers were also sunk. Ashore, there was heavy loss of life and widespread injury. The USA entered the war on the instant.

Japan seized Malaya (now Malaysia and Singapore) and Hong Kong, invaded Burma and was hell bent on the conquest of India (now India, Pakistan and Bangladesh). India had been under

Above: **A truly versatile transport, a C-47 fitted with floats, takes-off from a lake. These aircraft were not amphibians.** *(HG)*

Left: **Poised on mainwheels a C-47 performs a more conventional take-off.** *(JM)*

Above: Douglas DC-3's were built under licence before World War Two. This is an example manufactured in Japan by Showa as the L2D. Nakajima also produced the same model, the total being produced by both companies was around 570. (BR)

Aircraft deployed

	GB	Mid East	India	Total
Bombay (Bristol)	8	17		25
Dakota (Douglas)	2	7	12	21
DH86	6	1		7
Envoy (Airspeed)	5	2		7
Flamingo (DH)	6			6
Harrow (HP)	36			36
Hudson (Lockheed)	8			8
Lockheed 10/12	3	4	2	9
Petrel (Percival)	9	2		11
Valentia (Vickers)	12	2		14
TOTALS	69	56	19	44

Right: Consolidated C-87 Liberator Express, transport version of the famous B-24 Liberator bomber. (BR)

Above: **Curtiss C-46 Commando was powered by two 1700 hp Wright Double Row Cyclone R-2600-B 14-cylinder radial engines driving four-bladed propellers.** *(JM)*

British rule since 1857, but some of the native states had a certain measure of independence under British protection.

Britain had ruled Lower Burma since winning the Burmese war in 1852. She also took possession of Upper Burma in 1886. The whole country then became a mere province of British India. The British and Indian Army regiments facing the Japanese in Burma made a 200 mile (322km) fighting withdrawal to India that they completed by April 1942. They needed air support from transport squadrons in the evacuation of casualties. There were also British residents to be flown out as well as Burmese and other refugees.

Winston Churchill's War Cabinet was informed of the dearth of transport aircraft in the India/Burma theatre as their numbers stood on 1 April 1942. Even more than half a century later it makes the flesh crawl. One wonders about the quality of the Intelligence services that apparently had no inkling of Japan's intentions. The deprivation that this front had suffered was owed, of course, to the fact that it had seen no fighting yet and all attention was on North Africa, whither the bulk of equipment of every kind was directed. The information given to the cabinet about the number of transport aircraft available in the United Kingdom, Middle East and India was as follows.

BOMBAY: Troop carrier/bomber-transport. Entered service 1937. Crew 3, troops 24. Two 1010hp Bristol Pegasus XXII. Wingspan 95ft 9in (29.18m), length 69ft 3in (21.1m), height 19ft 11in 6.07m). Weight empty 13,800lb (6,260kg), loaded 20,000lb (9,072kg). Max speed 192mph (309km/h) at 6,500ft (1,980m). Range 880 miles (1,415km), with fuselage tanks 2,230 miles (3,588km).

DAKOTA. Developed as military transport from DC-3. First flew 1935. Glider tug, paratroop carrier, personnel transport, freighter, ambulance. Crew 3, troops 28. Two 1,200hp Pratt & Whitney Twin

Below: **A Chinese Nationalist Air Force C-46 Commando, one of the many nations which operated the aircraft after World War Two.**

Wasp engines. Wingspan 95ft (28.9m), length 64ft 6in (19.6m), height 16ft 11in (5.16m). Weight empty 16,865lb (7,650kg), loaded 25,200lb (11,430kg), 31,000lb (14,061kg) maximum. Max speed 230mph (370km/h) at 8,500ft (2,590m). Range 1,500 miles (2,125 miles (3,419km) max.

DE HAVILLAND 86B. Made its first flight in 1934 as a civil airliner. First two delivered to RAF in 1937 for communications duties and for training wireless operators. Four 200hp DH Gipsy Six engines. Max speed 166mph (267km/h), loaded weight 10,250lb (4,649kg). Range 450–750 miles (724–1,206km).

ENVOY. First flight 1934. Seven built for RAF. Two 350hp Armstrong Siddeley Cheetah engines. Loaded weight 6,600lb (2,993kg). Max speed 203mph (326km/h). Range 620 miles (997km).

FLAMINGO. Civil airliner, first flight December 1938. Two 930hp Bristol Perseus XVI engines. Loaded weight 17,600lb (7,983kg). Max speed 290mph (466km/h). Range 1,210 miles (1,947km).

HARROW. First flew October 1936. MkI had two 830hp Bristol Pegasus X engines, MkII had 925hp Pegasus XX. Carried 20 passengers. Two Harrows evacuated wounded men after Arnhem battle. Wingspan 88ft 5in (26.9m), length 82ft 2in (25m), height 19ft 5in (5.92m). Weight empty 13,600lb (6,169kg), loaded 23,000lb (10,433kg). Max speed 200mph (322km/h). Range 1,250 miles (2,011km).

HUDSON. Civil airliner Lockheed 14. First flight July 1937. MkI, two 1,100hp Wright Cyclone; MkVI two 1,200hp Pratt & Whitney Twin Wasp engines. Wingspan 65ft 6in (19.9m), length 44ft 4in (13.5m), height 11ft 10.5in (3.62m). Empty weight

Above: **Indian troops about to board a C-46 Commando in Burma. The USAAF flew many missions in support of the famous Chindits force.** *(BR)*

Right: **Shorts Sunderland flying boats were used, in World War Two, as maritime reconnaissance and anti-submarine attack aircraft. Towards the end of the war their role changed more to reconnaissance and transport. The aircraft shown is a Sunderland GR.V of No 230 Squadron RAF over Young Sound.** *(HC)*

Mk I 12,000lb (5,443kg), loaded 17,500lb (7,763kg), MkVI empty 12,992lb (5,893kg), loaded 17,500lb (7,763kg). Max speed MkI 246mph (396km/h), MkVI 284mph (457km/h). Range both marks 21,060 miles (33,885km).

LOCKHEED 12. Twin-engine low wing monoplane.

PETREL. RAF name for P16E MkV. Two 205hp Gipsy Six II engines. Loaded weight 5,550lb (2,517kg). Max speed 195mph (314km/h). Range 700 miles (1,126km).

VALENTIA. Delivered to RAF May 1934. Developed from Victoria troop-carrier. Crew 2, troops 22. Two 650hp Bristol Pegasus II ls or M3. Wingspan 87ft 4in (26.6m), length 56ft 9in 17.3m), weight empty 10,944lb (4,964kg), loaded 19,500lb (8,845kg). Max speed 120mph (193km/h). Range 800 miles (1,287km).

Since February 1942 a detachment of No 31 Squadron had been busy rescuing refugees with Valentias based at Akyab, in Burma, about 80 miles (130km) from the Indian frontier. The following month another detachment moved to Dinjan, in Assam, and in April the squadron began to take delivery of Dakotas. The refugees were assembling

at Myitkyina, some 170 miles (275km) from the safety of Assam. The Valentias and Dakotas had to cross the mountains in turbulent air and be on the lookout for Japanese fighters. The airfields at Akyab and Myitkyina were bombed, one Dakota was destroyed and another two were too badly damaged to fly.

The Japanese entered Myitkyina on 8 May. Now the Dakotas' errands of mercy changed from evacuating people to helping them, both military and refugees, by dropping food and other necessities at places on the route they were taking to the safety of India. There was a dearth of parachutes, so the same means to which No 30 Squadron had resorted when making supply drops to the Kut garrison 26 years earlier was adopted: free drops and optimism that the sacks would withstand the impact with the ground if two or three of them were used, one inside another.

Early in 1943 the retribution that Japan had invited by invading Burma began to take shape. Its organising genius and commander was Brigadier (later Major-General) Orde Wingate, whose unorthodox military tactics and eccentricities of character and appearance made him unique. Immensely experienced in guerrilla warfare, he had been been appointed by General Sir Archibald Wavell (who was promoted to Field Marshal in January 1943 and eventually elevated to the peerage) to form long-range penetration groups and harass the Japanese. Bearded, addicted to wearing an old-fashioned white military sun helmet of

Below: **Developed as a more powerful successor to the Wellington bomber, the Vickers Warwick never served in that role. It did however prove to be a valued transport. The version shown is equipped for air sea rescue (ASR).** *(BR)*

Right: **Shorts Sunderland III in RAF Transport Command service. The radio call sign 0QZF relates to: - O, Transport Command; Q, aircraft type and ZF, the operating squadron. This particular aircraft was loaned to British Overseas Airways as a Sandringham V.**
(BR)

ancient pattern, Wingate was also unique in possessing all the qualities that his new duties needed. The insignia he took for his command was the Chinthe, a fabulous animal and guardian of Burmese pagodas. This was soon corrupted to Chindit, and the force became famous as The Chindits. Eight Chindit columns set off for Burma in February.

Fifty miles (80km) east of Dacca, which is now the capital of Bangladesh, there is a town called Agartala. In February 1943 its aerodrome became the principal base from which the columns would be victualled and generally supplied. Here, Hudsons of No 194 Squadron and Dakotas of 31 were stationed. On February 14 and 15, escorted by Curtiss Mohawks of No 5 Squadron, 194 Sqdn made 10 supply sorties and by night on the 15th, 16th and 18th the same squadron and Dakotas of No 31 flew a total of 16. Eleven days later a Dakota managed to land on a clear area that was only about half a mile (0.8km) long and surrounded by 100ft (30m) trees. This took outstanding skill and the take-off, with 17 soldiers needing medical treatment, was equally difficult and dangerous.

The Mohawk, a little-known fighter, was delivered to the French Air Force in 1939. After France capitulated to the enemy, 100 Mohawks were diverted to the RAF and shipped between July and September 1940. Late the following year they were sent on to India and the Middle East. Nos 5, 146 and 155 RAF Squadrons and No 3 Squadron South African Air Force were given them.

The air supply demanded much flying of the highest quality. On 5 May Wingate thanked the RAF Headquarters:"Throughout the campaign has been nearly perfect and capable of astonishing performances. The men on the ground were first class. The W/T (wireless telegraphy) was as excellent as it was vital."

The scale of transport operations was not yet adequate. With the prospect of a long period of campaigning in Burma, Anglo-American Troop Carrier Command came into being on 15 December 1943, with an American commander, the USAAF's Brigadier-General William D. Old. One of its components was the RAF's No 177 Wing under Group Captain G.F. K. Donaldson, which consisted of four Dakota squadrons, Nos 31, 62, 117 and 194, each with 100 aircraft. Separately, No 353 Sqdn's Hudsons were busy over India, flying passengers and doing a chore that had so often thrust itself upon the RAF – carrying mail.

Arakan is the area of Burma about 200 miles (320km) wide and 450 miles (725km) long, between the Assam frontier in the north and the Irrawady delta in the south. It was there that the first offensive against the Japanese was made from December 1942 to May 1943. On 4 February 1944 the Japanese launched an offensive in the same area. The British and Indian Army defenders were hard pressed and nearly overrun, but the assiduous transport work of 177 Wing helped to repel the enemy.

Since Wingate's first venture into Burma his force had grown from two brigades to six, none of which was Indian Army, and he had received promotion to Major-General. He had been given his own air formation, based at Hailakand, in India and titled No 1 Air Commando Group. Its Commanding Officer was a 34-year-old American fighter ace, Colonel Philip G. Cochrane, and it comprised 11 USAAF squadrons, a mixture of glider tugs, bombers, fighters, light aircraft for casualty evacuation, training types and helicopters, of which the details are:

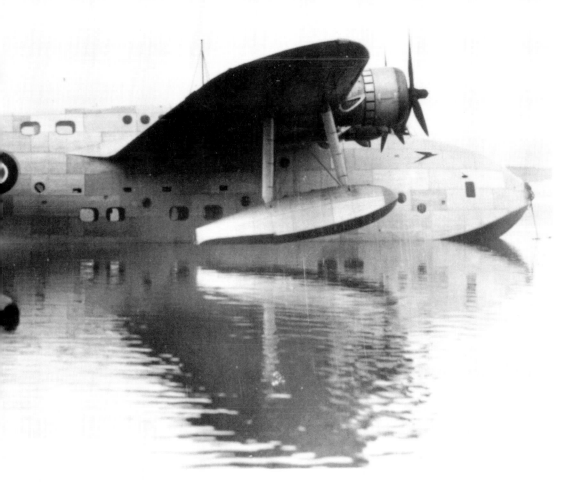

13 Douglas C-47	Skytrain transports
12 Noorduyn UC-64	Trainers
150 Waco CG4A	Hadrian gliders
75 Vultee TG5	Training gliders
100 Vultee L1	Vigilant light aircraft
100 Vultee L5	Sentinel light aircraft
6 Sikorsky YR4	Helicopters
30 North American P-51A Mustang	
	fighters
12 North American B-25H Mitchell	
	medium bombers

The time had come for another foray into Burma, in which 177 Wing was also to take part. The Long Range Penetration columns were to set off in Hadrian gliders on the evening of 5 March 1944. The plan, code-named Operation Thursday, called for the greatest number of gliders used to date on a single operation and was not exceeded until the Normandy invasion in 1944.

Landings were to be made on two cleared areas, code-named Piccadilly and Broadway, 20 miles (32km) apart and behind enemy lines, as the first move. Later landings would be made at a third, known as Chowringee (a street in Calcutta). Of the 12,000-strong force, 10,000 were to be transported by air. The aircraft taking part were stationed at Lalaghat, in Assam. A galaxy of anxious senior officers was assembled to see the first departures, most notably Lieutenant-General Sir William Slim

Above: **An RAF Lockheed Hudson departs the snow bound airfield of Evere, Belgium in January 1945. The Spitfire XVIE's are from No 421 'Red Indians' Squadron of the Royal Canadian Air Force.** *(HC)*

(later Field Marshal Lord), commanding the Fourteenth Army; an American, Lieutenant-General George Stratemeyer, commanding Western Air Command; and the AOC Troop Carrier Command, Air Vice Marshal Thomas Williams.

For communications the USAAF used the Vultee-Stinson Vigilant and Sentinel. The former had a 300hp Lycoming engine, its loaded weight was 3,322lb (1,509kg), max speed 123mph (198km/h), range 350 miles (563km), wingspan 51ft (15.5m), length 34ft (10.3m). The RAF used it for light liaison and artillery spotting. The latter aeroplane was powered by a 185hp Lycoming engine. Its loaded weight was 2,045lb (927kg), max speed 120mph (193km/h), wingspan 34ft (10.36m), length 24ft 2in (7.37m). In the RAF the aircraft served as a spotter and ambulance.

The arrival of one of these interrupted proceedings. Colonel Cochrane had had a hunch that the enemy might be keeping watch on Piccadilly, which had been used the year before for a Dakota to pick up wounded. He had ordered a last-minute photographic reconnaissance. The Vultee's pilot gave him a package of photographs just taken of Piccadilly. They showed that the enemy had laid tree trunks on Piccadilly. Because photo recce, or PR as the air forces called it, might alert the Japanese it had been forbidden for the past 48 hours, so this photography had not been overt, but combined with a bombing mission. Now the question to resolve was whether the enemy was aware of the planned operation. The decision was against this.

Take-off had been scheduled for 1740hrs.

Scrutinising and discussing the photos delayed it until 1812hrs, when the first Dakota was airborne towing a pair of Hadrians. By 2000hrs 25 more triple take-offs had been made. Soon the familiar cussedness of inanimate objects, in particular mechanical ones, cast doubts on the attendance of good fortune. One tug and its train had crashed before even getting airborne. Now more aeroplanes began returning because their tow ropes had broken; the gliders had forced-landed miles from where they should have. The next lot of Dakotas to set off towed only one glider. After them went the remainder, to drop their paratroops. Signals sent during the next few hours were confused or contradictory but it was eventually understood that 18 of the first lot of gliders had strayed. Of the second group, nine Dakotas and tugs were recalled. Some gliders crashed into trees, with the loss of 23 lives. However, 47 RAF and 36 USAAF Dakotas carried on. All of them set down on Broadway on the night of 6/7 March.

The night of 7/8 again witnessed mishaps. Of 44 sorties the RAF flew, 11 were aborted when 18 aircraft en route to Broadway received a recall: the landing ground was considered unsafe at night unless it was 4,000 yards (3,675m) long; it was only 2,700 (2,469m). The 11 who did not hear the signal landed safely nonetheless. By 11 March the Dakota sorties totalled 330. Of these the RAF had flown 74 to Chowringhee and to Broadway 257. The USAAF flew altogether 329. Total weight of supplies delivered was 509,083lb (230,920kg) and 1,359 mules were also carried.

This phase of the campaign ended with tragedy. A USAAF B-25 Mitchell (named after General Billy Mitchell, who in 1918 had proposed the first use of the air to position troops to attack an enemy's rear) crashed on the night of 24 March. Aboard it was Wingate. No-one survived. The wreckage was found within 48 hours but the cause of the accident was never solved.

Below: **A Lockheed Hudson III of the RAF, this aircraft was originally in US Navy service and carried the serial numbers 41- 23282.** *(BR)*

By the last week in May a new and accumulating difficulty had to be dealt with. The number of wounded and of men ill with pneumonia, typhoid, dysentery and malaria had grown to several hundred. They needed hospital treatment. The Chindits were now so far from the aerodromes in India that the Vigilant and Sentinel casualty evacuation aircraft could not reach them. The country was too swampy to permit the laying out of airfields that could take Dakotas. But there was a big lake at Indawgyi. The nearest flying boat squadron was stationed in Ceylon, 1,250 miles (2,010km) distant. Two of No

239 Squadron's Sunderlands were detailed to go to the rescue. First, on 27 May, one of them flew to Calcutta, where Imperial Airways C class Empire flying boats (from which the Sunderland was developed) had been landing on and taking off from the Hooghly river every week for years.

A hospital much closer than Calcutta had to be found. There was one at Dibrugarh on the Brahmaputra, between the Naga Hills to the south and the Mishmi Hills on the north. The distance from the lake to the hospital was only 200 miles (322km), but there were the swirling air currents

in the Ledo Pass and Japanese fighters patrolling.

On 1 June a Sunderland's first attempt to make the journey from the lake to Dibrugarh had to be abandoned when at 20,000ft (6,096m) it was still in cloud. A day later it made the complete journey in an hour and a half, with 32 patients: not a full load, because it had to make 10,000 ft (3,050m). The day after that there were 36 patients on board. Enemy fighters were seen, so next day four Mustangs gave escort and 39 patients were flown to Assam. On 5 June two sorties enabled 81 to be lifted out of Burma. The second Sunderland arrived the

following day. Despite adverse weather the flying boats persisted, until by 4 July 509 patients had been conveyed in 14 sorties. On that last day, high wind capsized one Sunderland at its moorings on the river and it sank.

The Short Sunderland was designed to be a long-range general reconnaissance and anti-submarine flying boat with a crew of 13. It entered RAF service in 1938 with No 230 Squadron in Singapore and No 210 at Pembroke Dock. The power plants were four 1,200hp Pratt and Whitney Twin Wasp R-1830. Its wingspan was 112ft 9½in

Right: **WACO CG-13A cargo and troop carrying glider, built by The WACO Aircraft Company of Troy, Ohio.** *(HG*

(34.38m), length 85ft 4in (26m), height 32ft 10½in (10.02m), empty weight 37,000lb (16,783kg), loaded 60,000lb (27,216kg). Max speed 213mph (343km/h), range 2,980 miles (4,795km).

The Japanese had fought their way into India and two towns were under siege: Kohima, 30 miles (48km) inside the frontier, and Imphal, 65 miles (105km) to the south and also 30 miles (48km) deep into Assam. The Allies' 5th Indian Division was to be transferred from the Arakan front to Imphal. This movement would be the biggest ever made by air. It was started on 19 March by 15 RAF Dakotas and 20 C-46s of the USAAF. Over 10 days these completed the transfer in 758 sorties. From Imphal 35,000 wounded, sick and non-combatants were also evacuated.

From the Middle East 15 Dakotas of 216 Sqdn and 64 USAAF Dakotas were detached to take part in the delivery of supplies and troop movements and remained until the middle of June. Between 18 April and 30 June, 300 aircraft supplied Imphal with 23,500 tons of materiel.

The Douglas C-46 troop and cargo transport prototype appeared in 1940. Its wingspan was 108ft 1in (39.9m), length 76ft 4in (23.2m), height 21ft 9in (6.6m). Empty weight 29,483lb (1,3373kg), loaded weight 50,000lb (22,680kg). Cruising speed 227mph (465km/h), range 1,699 miles (2,733km).

Above: **The WACO CG-4A assault glider was not only produced by WACO but 14 other companies in the United States. Over 20,400 were produced, serving with the US Army as the CG-4A Haig and with the RAF as the Hadrian.** *(HC)*

CHAPTER SEVEN

Airborne Assault

We approached the coast at 3,000 to 4,000ft,
in the light Flak range. To hit the slipstream of the aircraft
in front was terrifying. When the gliders cast off a
few miles from the coast, it was bedlam.

The most valuable tactical principle learned during the first four years and nine months of the Second World War was probably that an assault should be led by airborne troops.

This form of attack superseded even the surprise sprung by the German Army and Air Force with their combined assaults on Poland in 1939 and France in 1940: the Blitzkrieg, the lightning war in which dive bombers and tanks co-ordinated their attacks. Its audacity shocked the armies of every other country in the world. The innovation that crushed Poland in 33 September and October days in 1939 surprised them even more than the invasions of Norway, Denmark, Belgium and Holland would in 1940. They had known for at least six years that the Russians had trained thousands of parachute troops; but the Germans had not demonstrated the Blitzkrieg to the military attachés in Berlin.

At first the parachute and gliderborne attacks made a lesser impact than the Blitzkrieg. The airborne strikes of 1939 were on a much smaller scale than the Germans' invasion of France in 1940. No other nation emulated, on the same scale, the German tactic that had conquered the French Army and forced the British to retreat. In a lesser way, during the Allied invasion of France in 1944 when the Germans blocked the advance at Falaise, the British and American armour went in supported by ground-attack fighters in a small-scale Blitz that did terrible execution.

By the time the Allies launched their invasion of France on the night of 5/6 June 1944 it was an established military principle that airborne troops must be the spearhead of any attack. The invading forces by air, land and sea were fortified by the first essential requirement for such an operation – air supremacy. The air marshals, generals and admirals who, with their staffs, had planned the invasion, provided the other essential – misdirection. By every possible ingenious means the defending enemy was deluded into deciding that the invasion, which they knew must be imminent, would be launched at the coast in the Calais area, where the sea crossing would be the shortest possible. The fourth *sine qua non* was the weather. Luck was on the Allies' side: it was fine and the forecast was accurate.

Nos 38 and 46 Groups of RAF Transport Command comprised 15 squadrons numbering 400 aircraft to drop 7,000 paratroops over Normandy. A few minutes before midnight on 5 June 1944, 750 members of the Parachute Regiment's 9th Battalion dropped into France from 300 Dakotas. Their objective was the gun battery at Merville, on the Normandy coast, whose guns were sighted to fire across the Orne estuary and bombard the beaches where the British and Canadians were to land.

It was not an accurate drop. Low-cover radar and the roar of aero engines warned the enemy in time for the Flak batteries and machine guns to put up a withering barrage. Some of the Dakotas missed their dropping zone and had to go round again. A stick of 20 men needed at least 45 seconds to leave an aircraft. The buffeting of exploding shells and banking to turn threw the paratroops about and

delayed their exits. Flying at two miles a minute 3.2km/h), they were widely scattered. To make it worse the enemy had flooded the marshland around the estuary of the River Dives. Only 150 of the attackers made the rendezvous. Four gliders carrying essential equipment were missing and three gliders who should have crash-landed right onto the battery position came to ground on the outskirts. The small number that had come down at more or less the right place stormed the battery and captured it in 20 minutes of fighting that left only 65 of them to carry on.

The first member of the Allied forces to land in Normandy on D-Day itself, 6 June 1944, was Lieutenant Bobby de la Tour of the Parachute Regiment. He commanded a stick of ten Pathfinders whose task was to lay out lights in a small field to guide the following waves of parachute and glider-borne troops of the British 6th Airborne Division. A few months earlier he had been acting in a musical comedy in London.

He was flown into battle by Flight Lieutenant Oliver Kingdon (later OBE, DFC) of No 295 Squadron. There were six Albemarles on this operation, three of 295 Sqn based at Harwell and three of 296 based at Brize Norton. They were the first to cross the enemy-occupied coast in the battles to liberate Europe. All the crews had been chosen for their outstanding skill at accurate navigation and flying. Kingdon's navigator, Sergeant Muddiman, had exceptional night vision and map-reading skills. He guided his pilot on the last few

thousand yards and gave the signal for the paratroops to jump so as they would land on precisely the right spot. Oliver Kingdon recalls, "We crossed the coast near Ouistrehem in pale moonlight and, using the aerial photographs which we had been studying for many hours, flew at 500ft (152m) to the small field which had been designated our dropping zone. Then came a message on the intercom that the sergeant who was to jump last had fouled his lines and had not gone. I told the crew we would go round again and our excellent map-reader navigated us back over the same field and the sergeant jumped. We heard later that Bobby de la Tour had been killed in action two weeks after the landing."

Of the three 296 Squadron Albemarles that had taken off an hour before midnight, the leading one was flown by a flight commander, Squadron Leader Leonard Archer (later Wing Commander DSO OBE AFC). The paratroops aboard were to blow up gun emplacements and lay a flare path to guide the glider tugs to their landing zone.

Leonard Archer recalls, "We approached the French coast in a dark, overcast sky, hoping we could see enough features to pinpoint our position. All the crew knew the route by heart: up to 5,000ft (1,525m) over coastal light Flak, skirt the canal, cross it to the north, over Ouistrehem reduce height to 1,000 ft (305m), speed 140 knots, pick up small lake, prepare to jump. Navigator to get us to the dropping zone (DZ), the gunner vigilant for opposition, wireless op helping the departing guests, and the pilot obeying orders for height, speed and

Above: **Main assault glider of the Luftwaffe, the DFS230A-1 could carry 10 fully-equipped infantry soldiers. On 20 May 1941, Germany launched Operation Mercury to seize the island of Crete. A force of 80, DFS.230's were deployed to secure Maleme airfield on the morning of the attack.** *(HC)*

Above: **The Gotha Go242 assault glider was that company's main product of World War Two. The two-wheeled dolly undercarriage was jettisoned after take-off.** *(HC)*

Above right: **Britain's main assault glider the Airspeed AS.51 Horsa could carry up to 25 fighting troops. A total of 3655 were built.** *(HC)*

Far right: **Conceived originally as an assault glider the General Aircraft Hotspur was deemed too small for that purpose. It was however used very successfully as a trainer.** *(HC)*

direction. ".... On track and our DZ identified ahead. All is quiet and we warn the passengers. Height 600ft (183m) ... open hatch... adjust speed to 120 knots, on goes the red light and slight bumps are felt as the troops leave the aircraft."

The flight nearly ended then. Another Albemarle flying at the same height and speed loomed almost in the same airspace. "By instinct I kicked the big aircraft hard over almost onto its back and missed by a hair's breadth," Archer relates. The last passenger – the officer commanding the stick – was thrown back into the aeroplane and onto its roof as it rolled. The pilot circled and the stick commander jumped as Flak began to burst all around.

Aircraft Squadrons deployed on Operation Mallard

SQDN	AIRCRAFT	NUMBER	AIRFIELD
48	Dakota & Horsa	22	Down Ampney
190	Stirling & Horsa	18	Fairford
196	Stirling & Horsa	17	Keevil
271	Dakota & Horsa	15	Down Ampney
295	Albemarle & Horsa	20	Harwell
296	Albemarele & Horsa	20	Brize Norton
297	Albemarle & Horsa	20	Brize Norton
298	Halifax & Horsa	1	Tarrant Rushton
298	Halifax & Hamilcar	15	Tarrant Rushton
299	Stirling & Horsa	18	Keevil
512	Stirling & Horsa	18	Broadwell
570	Albemarle & Horsa	20	Harwell
575	Dakota & Horsa	18	Broadwell
620	Stirling & Horsa	18	Fairford
644	Halifax and Horsa	1	Tarrant Rushton
644	Halifax & Hamilcar	18	Tarrant Rushton

The total numbers of tugs and gliders were:
80 Albemarles, 73 Dakotas, 32 Halifaxes, 71 Stirlings, 226 Horsas, 30 Hamilcars.

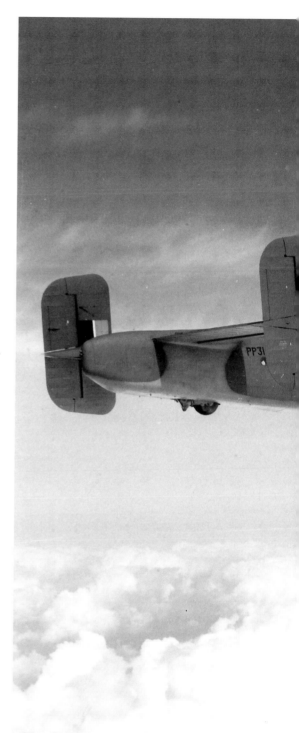

Above: **Percival Proctor IA's were used by the RAF as communications aircraft. After World War Two many were purchased by amateur pilots and newly born flying clubs.** *(BR)*

On the following evening the six Albemarle crews of Nos 295 and 296 Squadrons who had been the first over France took part in Operation Mallard, a massive display of air strength involving 16 squadrons. The tugs were Albemarles, Dakotas, Halifaxes and Stirlings; the gliders were Horsas and Hamilcars; the airfields from which they took off were Down Ampney, Fairford, Keevil, Harwell, Brize Norton, Tarrant Rushton and Broadwell.

This aerial armada comprised 256 combinations of tugs and glider. So many aircraft flying with scant separation between them, both laterally and horizontally, the air agitated by slipstreams as well as the natural eddying air currents of a warm day, made flying difficult and dangerous with a high collision risk. Despite this a magnificent feat of airmanship was accomplished: 246 gliders (96.09 per cent) landed successfully.

Leonard Archer says about this operation: "In the afternoon of the sixth of June we took off, formed up and headed for the coast. The lead aircraft flew for half the time it took the whole lot to become airborne. Then the formation flew over the airfield as the last one took off. It was all quite orderly until we reached the Channel, when, for some reason, everyone crowded up and one couldn't move up, down or sideways. This was the worst part of the operation. I think we must have joined a formation from another base. We approached the coast at 3,000 to 4,000ft (915 to 1,290m), in the light Flak range. To hit the slipstream of the aircraft in front was terrifying. When the gliders cast off a few miles over the coast it was bedlam. The tow ropes were still attached to the aeroplanes and you got mixed up with the gliders in front as they lost speed. It was a great relief to part with your glider, dive low, cast off the tow rope and head for home. The fighters were above us, keeping the hostile fighters away. They did it well, for our losses were small. The later airborne assaults were quite different, more orderly, more strung out and making deeper penetration over enemy territory." The crowded take-off was necessary because the airborne troops had to arrive over the target as close together as possible, the formation was therefore restricted to a narrow corridor and the journey was short.

Flight Lieutenant G. L. (Lee) Wilson won his DFC on Mallard. Taking off, he had great difficulty in avoiding collisions with the glider immediately ahead and the tugs astern and on both sides. It was only a little less difficult to keep station when airborne, with one's wing tips only a few feet clear of the aeroplanes to port and starboard. Even when

there is plenty of room, aircraft are tossed about by up-draughts and down-draughts. The whole formation was at 1,500ft (475m). Near the dropping zone the tug would descend steeply to 150ft (45m) and when the glider pilot identified his dropping zone he would release the cable. The aeroplane would then turn to starboard.

Lee Wilson says, "I had a very conscientious pilot flying the Horsa. He kept saying he couldn't see the DZ. When he eventually let go and I turned, we flew right over a Flak tower from which 20mm Oerlikons focused their attention on us. Both engines caught fire and the aircraft was riddled. One engine was failing while I climbed to 1,100ft (335m)."

He forced his crew to bale out, then followed them, landed on the roof of a cottage and fell through into the attic. His leg was bleeding and he found when he eventually returned to base that he had broken the fibula. Meanwhile he was on the ground in the midst of a battle. A tank picked him up and

Above: **The Handley Page Halifax C.VIII was the unmanned transport version of the Halifax Bomber. It could carry 8000 lbs (3629 kgs) of cargo or 11 passengers.** *(BR)*

Above: **Designed originally as a bomber, the Armstrong Whitworth AW.41 Albemarle was constructed mainly from steel and wood. Only 32 were completed as bombers and later converted to transports. In total 600 were built. The aircraft shown is the STV, glider tug in service with No 297 Squadron RAF.** *(BR)*

deposited him at a mobile field hospital; which consisted of one tent and one Army doctor with some nursing orderlies. Thence he was put aboard a landing ship, and taken back to England.

The Armstrong Whitworth Albemarle was one of the lesser-known aeroplanes. Only Nos 295, 296, 297 and 570 Squadrons flew them in Britain, while in North Africa they were flown by Nos 296, 297, 161 and 511.

Although the first 32 were built as bombers, none ever operated in this role. After numerous modifications they eventually became glider tugs and special transport to the airborne forces.

The first squadron to get them was 295, in January 1943. They were first used as glider tugs in the invasion of Sicily. The twin engines were 1590hp Bristol Hercules XI. Wingspan was 77ft (23.4m), length 59ft 11in (18.26m), height 15ft 7in (4.75m). Loaded weight was 22,600lb (10,251kg). Max speed 265mph (426km/h). Range 1,300 miles (2,092km). Twin hand-operated Vickers K guns were mounted amidships.

Operation Dragoon

Operation Dragoon, the invasion of southern France on 15 August 1944, is seldom given the recognition it deserves for making the first attack on a new front in the south of France. It drew little public attention compared with the intense interest in the progress of the battles in northern France. The Dragoon landings were made on the coast between Toulon and Cannes. Although the German 13th Army, holding the area, consisted of seven second-rate infantry divisions and a better quality, but not the best, Panzer division, the thrust towards the north and east was no sinecure. In the forefront of the attack were 9,732 parachute and gliderborne troops.

Left: **An ex-Eastern Air Lines Douglas DC-2 in Australian Service. The location is No. 2 Wireless Air Gunners school based at Parkes, NSW, Australia. This aircraft crashed on 8 January 1942 but was rebuilt and entered on the civil register in 1945 as VH-CRG.** (BR)

Right: **Three Airspeed Horsas take-off in formation. These are MkI versions having a towing bracket under each wing necessitating the use of a bifurcated rope. The Mk II had a single towing socket under the nose. Early wire tow ropes were replaced, in 1944, by types made from nylon.** *(HC)*

when the tow rope was cast off, was 1 in 13 and, with full flap at 90 knots, 1 in 1.5; towed at 145 knots, the clean stall occurred at 52 knots and with full flap at 43 knots.

At 1100hrs on 24 March the glider pilots approaching their landing zone found the air obscured by smoke and dust rising from the town of Wesel, which had been bombed and was burning. The explosions of heavy Flak were tossing them about and the light Flak came sizzling up in multi-coloured streaks of tracer. The drifting miasma created by the bombing obscured the ground. A hundred knots was too fast for landing, but putting on flap would steepen the descent and plunge the gliders into the murk. The landing caused 25 per cent casualties, most of them not fatal or serious, and 80 per cent of the gliders were destroyed or damaged. After six days on the ground, the pilots were flown back to England. Those who did not return until a few days after they had landed in the

battle area were flown home via the RAF station at Down Ampney, in Gloucestershire, where there was a Customs post. They had been abroad, some for six or seven days, so of course they had to satisfy the officials that they had nothing to declare!

Among those who played a dangerous and surreptitious part in Varsity was an officer of the Women's Auxiliary Air Force. At RAF Station Earls Colne there were four Intelligence officers: a squadron leader, two flying officers and their equivalent in rank, a WAAF, Section Officer Rosemary Britten. As the forthcoming airborne assault was presumed to be the war's last, all three of the junior officers were keen to participate. The Station Commander, a group captain, agreed that the toss of a coin should decide who it was to be. In the squadron leader's presence, one of the male officers won but ceded his place to the lady. This was not divulged to the group captain. The squadron leader I. O. confided it to 296 (Halifax) Squadron's

Below: **The Miles Messenger was in production before World War Two as a four-seat light touring aircraft. At the outbreak of war those civilian aircraft were requisitioned, whilst Miles continued production for the RAF. The aircraft was used for communication purposes, one being the personal aircraft of Field Marshall Montgomery during the D-Day Landings.** *(BR)*

Above: **The Lockheed C-69 Constellation entered service with US Army Air Transport service on 17 April 1944 when it was flown non-stop from Burbank, California to Washington DC, in 7 hrs 3 min.** *(Lockheed)*

Right: **A US Navy Beechcraft JRB-1 Expeditor, twin-engined light transport.** *(JM)*

335624

Above: **First flown on 5 July 1942 the Avro 685 York was a direct descendant of the famous Lancaster bomber. The York carried a crew or four and up to 24 passengers. The aircraft shown is 'Ascalon' used by Winston Churchill.** *(BR)*

Left: **Rear view of a Beechcraft Expeditor, this is a US Army UC-45A.** *(BR)*

Above: **Cessna T-50, a twin-engined utility aircraft used by the US Army as a trainer AT-17 Bobcat or as a light transport UC-78 Brasshat. The RCAF used it as an advanced trainer named Crane from 1941 in the Empire Flying Schools.** *(BR)*

Right: **Noorduyn C-64 Norseman of the USAF in Normandy invasion markings.** *(JM)*

Below: **The prototype of the Airspeed AS.10 Oxford first flew on 19 June 1937 with a few production aircraft reaching airlines before World War Two. At the outbreak of war the Oxford was adopted by the RAF as a multi-engine trainer and communications aircraft. Over 8500 were built and were also used by the Empire Flying Schools for training aircrews. The Oxford was retired from service in 1954.** *(JM)*

C. O., a wing commander, who nominated one of the most reliable crews, whose pilot was Flying Officer Lamshed, to take Flight Officer Britten as supernumerary.

On the day preceding the operation the station abounded with VIPs, among them Air Chief Marshal Sir Arthur (later Lord) Tedder, General Eisenhower's Deputy Supreme Commander, and Sir Archibald Sinclair, Secretary of State for Air. It was important for Rosemary Britten to keep out of their way.

Next morning the crews were called at 0315 and breakfasted at 0415. She wore her oldest trousers and tunic and took her identity card, and the standard issue escape kit – plus powder and a lipstick. Crew members carried her life jacket and parachute. She walked with them to the aircraft, hoping it would be assumed that she was merely going to watch the take-off, got aboard unseen and hid there until dawn broke and the squadrons took off.

On the way, the air was crowded by Halifaxes towing Horsas, Dakotas towing pairs of Wacos, Dakotas returning after having released their tows over the landing zones, and RAF and USAF fighters. They crossed the Rhine into Germany. Hamminkeln and their glider's landing zone came in sight. The glider was released and disappeared from sight in the smoke. Rosemary Britten saw a Halifax going down in flames and only three parachutes following it. She saw a Hamilcar disintegrate, its passengers and a tank hurled out.

Flying Officer Lamshed turned for home. An

Right: **Soviet licence built Douglas DC-3 manufactured by Lisunov as the Li-2. They built more then 3500, all powered by licence built 1000 hp Wright R-1820 Cyclone nine-cylinder radial engines, designated M-62JR by the Shevetsov design bureau.** *(BR)*

Britain and the Middle East and Far East had to be handed over to civil airlines.

The first phase, which covered the period to the end of September, was an emergency method of coping with the problems of supply until other means of communication could be restored. Berlin had adequate stocks of food and coal which would, with the airlift, sustain existence. The main object of the second phase, covering October 1948 to February 1949, was to bring in enough supplies to prevent excessive hardship to the indigenous population in the coldest season of the year. The months December to February were the most critical. The number of aircraft available in the three immediately previous months had not been sufficient to build stocks. Winter weather was increasing the rate of consumption. It was also reducing the number of flights, but they continued by day and night.

One of the problems created by the weather was the effect of wind speed and direction. The Skymasters had a tricycle undercarriage, which gave them a great degree of immunity from the effect of cross-winds. None of the RAF aeroplanes, however, had this type of "undercart".

At first, four airfields in the Western Zone were used. Flights were along four 20-mile (32km) wide corridors that had been agreed by all four Allied countries at the war's end. All these air corridors converged on the Gatow airfield in West Berlin. Since Russia's closure of the road, rail and water routes into Berlin, Gatow's runway had been

lengthened to 2,000 yards (1,828m) and the hard standing area quadrupled. New airfields were built in the British Zone at Fassberg and in the French sector of Berlin at Tegel. Scrupulous being a word that did not figure in the USSR's attitude, the Kremlin warned the Americans, British and French that Soviet Air Force aeroplanes would be conducting exercises in all four corridors. They had no right to do so, for this had been forbidden when the corridors were established. Protests were met by further belligerence: Russia now threatened that the whole question of corridors would have to be reviewed. The RAF, representing the Allied Control Commission, retorted that the four-power agreement could not be altered and if Russia did announce a change in the rules the other powers would ignore it.

The three Western powers, unintimidated, increased the scale of activity by adding 70 more C-54s to the strength, which made the total 130. RAF Sunderlands joined the mixed fleet of aircraft and ferried between Finkenwerder and West Berlin's Havel Lake. Converted Halifax bombers known as Haltons, Tudors and 39 Lancastrian tankers, a transport variant of the Lancaster, owned by Flight Refuelling Ltd, joined the airlift. There was also an assortment of nine types of aircraft owned by British European Airways and 26 small charter companies. The objective was set at 750 tonnes a day but by 1 August 1948 the daily average was 2,250 tonnes, delivered in 215 British and 285 American sorties.

Major-General William H. Tunner, USAF, who

Above: **Four of Flight Refuelling Limited's (FRL) nine Avro Lancastrian (civilianised version of the Lancaster) tanker aircraft, which were used to fly fuel in to the city of Berlin during the Airlift which began on 27 July 1948 to end on 10 August 1949. FRL's aircraft carried a total of 6,975,021 gals (31,708,445.5 ltr) of fuel to Berlin; flight time was a total of 11672.21 hours and the distance flown 1,714,596 statute miles.** *(CC)*

Right: **A Handley Page Hastings C.MkI transport being loaded. Attached to underside mounts, is a Land Rover vehicle which will be air dropped in a forward combat area.** *(MOD)*

Below: **Hastings C.Mk I & II were used during the Berlin Airlift. This C.Mk II is being towed on to the flight ramp ready for operations.** *(MOD)*

had directed the Hump flights from August 1944 to the end, was appointed to command the airlift. To increase efficiency he reduced the number of flying hours done by each crew. Flying day and night, often in appalling weather, was brave and dedicated, but ultimately self-defeating. Frequency of deliveries was the most significant factor in the many facets of the operation, but weariness brought a decrease in efficiency as well as added danger.

One of the side benefits evolved by the operation was the modernisation of the Ground Controlled Approach system, which hitherto was installed only on commercial airfields and took 15 to 20 minutes to land an aircraft. The USAF Military Air Transport

Service delivered the necessary equipment to Gatow and Tegel. As both controllers and pilots began to become more skilled at using the system, landing times under control were reduced to three minutes and by the end of December more GCA approaches and landings were being made daily at Berlin than the total at all the airports in the USA.

By the end of 1948 the South African, New Zealand and Australian Air Forces had crews flying on the airlift. The bulk of the work was done by 200 C-54s, 40 Yorks, 40 Dakotas, and 15 Hastings, which had entered squadron service in October. By this time there were eight all-weather dispatch airfields and deliveries of 8,000 tonnes a day were

Above: **This Douglas R4D-8 is one of 100 R4D5/6 modified with wings of increased sweepback.** *(BR)*

Right: **Flight Refuelling Limited's Lancastrian downloading fuel at Tegel in blockaded Berlin. All FRL's Lancastrians were beautifully maintained and painted in distinctive 'Cobham Blue' colour scheme.** *(CC)*

Above: **Flight Refuelling's busy operations and briefing room at their site on Fulsbuttel airfield in Allied occupied Germany.** *(CC)*

Right: **Two Avro Yorks of the RAF taxi out from Wunstorf; in the background is an Avro Tudor belonging to an unidentifiable civil operator.** *(MOD)*

commonplace. The record was set on 16 April 1949 when 12,840 tonnes were landed.

Russia, recognising that not even the greatest obstacles it could inflict on its three former allies would deter them, threw in the towel. On 11 May 1949 it ended its blockade.

The airfields and the aircraft that used them were, in the British Zone: Wunstorf, by RAF Yorks and civilian tankers and freighters; Lubeck, by RAF Dakotas; Schleswigland, by RAF Hastings and civilian tankers; Fuhlsbuttel, by civilian freighters and tankers; Celle, by USAF Skymasters; Fassberg, by Skymasters. In the American Zone there were: Rhein-Main, by Skymasters; and Wiesbaden, by Skymasters.

The total weight of loads flown into Berlin by the RAF, USAF and civil aircraft was 2,325,808.7 tonnes. Of this, 1,586,000 were coal and 538,016 food. The RAF's contribution was 395,509 tonnes

Left: **Douglas C-74 Globemaster I note the two separate side-by-side pilot cockpits.** *(HG)*

Below: **Douglas C-124 Globemaster II a complete redesign of the C-74 shown above.** *(HG)*

Right: **Designed as a logistics transport for the USAF the Douglas C-133 Cargomaster could carry all the bulky loads which could not be loaded into the C-124. The C-133B was specifically designed to carry Thor, Minuteman and other ballistic missiles to bases throughout the United States and also to Europe. Power was supplied by four 7000/7500 hp Pratt & Whitney T-34 turboprop engines.** *(HG)*

Below: **The C-131 is the military version of the Convair Airliner. The C-131A is a casualty evacuation and cargo transport based on the model 240, whilst the C-131B carries out the same tasks it is based on the model 340.** *(JM)*

Left: **Douglas built over 200 of the military version of the DC-6, most went to the USAF's Military Air Transport Service (MATS) as the C-118. The US Navy operated it as the R6D.** *(HG)*

Right: **The Military Air Transport Service of the USAF operated the Lockheed C-121 Constellation for many years. The types used were the C-121A the military cargo version of the model 749; VC-121B military VIP transport version of the model 749 and the C-121C military transport version of the model 1049B. The US Navy operated Constellations as the R7V-1, military transport version of the model 1049B and the R7V-2 which differed from all other Constellations by being powered by four Pratt & Whitney T-34 turboprop engines.** *(Lockheed)*

Below: **Starting life as the Boeing 377 Stratocruiser a military C-97 transport version was soon developed.** *(JM)*

Left: **Designed originally by the Chase Aircraft Company Inc as the MS-8 Avitruk (flown in three distinct forms - as a glider, with two piston engines and with two turbojets) production and development was taken over by Fairchild. The resulting aircraft became the C-123 Provider, a true military transport workhorse.** *(JM)*

Below: **Dassault MD.315 Flamant light transports were built in quantity between 1947 and 1953 for the French Air Force. Two other versions were built; the 311 a bombing, navigation and photography trainer and the 312 a furnished six-seat military liaison aircraft. All versions were powered by two 580hp Renault 12502-201 inverted V-12 air-cooled engines.** *(JM)*

Left: **The Antonov An-2 was designed to the specification of the Soviet Ministry of Agriculture and Forestry under the designation Skn-1 and was first flown in 1947. Later officially designated An-2 it was used in large numbers by the Soviet armed forces, and the national airline Aeroflot. The An-2 was also exported to all of the Eastern bloc states and was manufactured under licence in Poland and China.** *(JM*

Below: **Piaggo began flight testing the P.136, amphibious seaplane on 29 August 1948. It was certificated in late 1949 and in 1950 the Italian military ordered 18 aircraft.** *(JM)*

Right: **Hunting Pembroke C.Mk54, a total of 33 were supplied to the West German Air Force.** *(JM)*

Right: **Scottish Aviation Twin Pioneer's were supplied to the RAF, as CC MkI (33) CC Mk2 (4) and CC Mk3(3), and were used as supply aircraft in Malaya.** *(JM)*

Below: **A De Havilland Sea Heron operated by the Fleet Air Arm (Royal Navy) as a shore-based communications aircraft.** *(BR)*

plus 167,000 passengers and 34,000 tonnes of mail and manufactured goods flown out of Berlin.

The benefit to the USA, Britain and France had extended beyond the actual flying. It included advancement in, and the acquisition of, a greater knowledge of science, administrative planning and improvisation.

Among those who were awarded decorations for their part in the great airlift was the RAF's Flight Lieutenant Roy Mather, who won the Air Force Cross for making more flights than any other pilot. There was an amusing corollary to this. A story circulated in the RAF that, when the operation was suspected to be approaching its end, he was told by a very senior officer that his tally of flights was less than that of the American pilot with the highest score, so he must put in even more hours and surpass it. The tale goes that his extra effort was in fact superfluous, as he had already passed the latter's total, for the USAF counted a return trip as two flights, whereas in the RAF it was one.

The Mediterranean, Middle East and Africa

When Britain annexed Cyprus in 1914 she apparently did not foresee its potential for civil war; which is surprising in view of her long colonial experience and the vastness of her heterogeneous empire. The Cypriots of Greek origin, who belonged to the Orthodox Church, numbered 80 per cent of the population; the other 20 per cent, Turkish Cypriots, were Muslims. It was an explosive combination. A small country inhabited by two races speaking different languages and practising

Below: **Flying over a devastated industrial area in the Berlin air corridor, a Lancastrian tanker of Flight Refuelling Limited carries its load of fuel onwards to Tegal airfield.** *(CC)*

Right: **The Canadair C-54-GM North Star military transport was almost redesigned of the Douglas C-54 Skymaster. It was powered by four Rolls-Royce Merlin 620 engines instead of Pratt & Whitney radials.** *(BR)*

Above: **Northrop's all-metal trimotor the C-125A Raider was ordered by the USAF. Twenty-three were built; 13 as assault transports and 10 as Arctic rescue aircraft equipped with ski-landing gear.** *(HC)*

different religions, products of mutually unsympathetic cultures, was an obvious breeding ground for civil war.

In the early 1950s, Britain began making her main base on the island. The Greek Cypriots resented the British presence in general and especially the enlargement of RAF and Army installations. They wanted union with Greece, which was reciprocated. Archbishop Makarios and Colonel Grivas became the leaders of this political movement, with its urban terrorists and guerrilla

force. Helicopters played an important part in internal security. No 244 Squadron's Sycamores were able to lift three armed men at a time and land them in the mountains, which rose to 5,000 ft (1,525m). This was made possible by removing every ounce of unnecessary weight and hovering above the ground cushion that affected operations at high altitude, while the passengers slid down a 30ft (9.1m) rope, which was then jettisoned. This feat was a useful innovation with many practical applications.

Eventually, after much bloodshed and destruction, a treaty was reached in 1959 making Cyprus an independent sovereign republic except for an area around the RAF airfield at Akrotiri and the Army base at Dhekelia.

Diplomatic bungling by the British government, which ignored the advice of the Chiefs of Staff that diplomacy, not military intervention, should be used to deal with a sudden crisis in the Middle East, resulted in a shoddy task being thrust on the British and French airborne forces: the attack on the Suez Canal Zone of Egypt in 1956.

That country, a British protectorate, had been a Sultanate and became a Kingdom in 1922. The Suez Canal, opened in 1869, was built under the supervision of a Frenchman, Ferdinand de Lesseps. In 1875 Britain obtained a controlling interest in it by buying all the shares owned by the Khedive

Above: **Vickers Valetta C. MkI, developed from the civil Viking IB, was a multi-purpose military transport.** *(MOD)*

Left: **The Max Holste MH.1521 was a six-seat general purpose aircraft powered by 450hp Pratt & Whitney R-985-AM-1 radial engine.** *(JM)*

Below: **Fairchild C-82A Packet military transport.** *(BR)*

Above: **The prototype of the Sud-Ouest SO.95 Corse II was first flown in World War Two after being designed and developed by the Groupe Technique de Cannes. It was ordered by the French military in 1945, as a light transport carrying a crew of two and up to 13 passengers.** *(BR)*

Above: **SNCASO (Sud-Ouest) SO-30P Bretagne was originally designed during World War Two in unoccupied France. The aircraft shown is a VIP transport version for the Aeronavale-French naval air arm.** *(BR)*

Left: **Avions Marcel Dessault supplied a large number of MD315 Flamant light transports to the French military services.** *(BR)*

(Governor) and in 1882 stationed troops in Egypt.

In 1952 senior Egyptian Army officers staged a coup d'état and exiled the king. In 1954 Colonel Nasser became Prime Minister and chairman of the revolutionary committee. He at once obtained an agreement with Britain that all British forces were to leave Egypt within 20 months. This departure was completed in April 1956. In July the USA and Britain withdrew their financial support for the construction of the Aswan High Dam on the Nile. A week later, Nasser proclaimed the nationalisation of the Universal Suez Canal Company and the seizure of its funds.

Britain, France and Israel would not tolerate this action, particularly as there was a danger that Russia would intervene militarily and cut off the route by which oil from the Persian Gulf was shipped to the West. Plans were made for a joint attack by Britain and France.

Israel precipitated Anglo-French action by striking first. Without giving any indication of their intention by reconnaissance flights, the Israeli Air Force went straight in on the evening of 29/30 October. To the east of the canal lie low, sandy hills which are crossed by a road through the Mitla Pass, which the Israelis intended to occupy. Here, 16 Dakotas dropped 395 paratroops at 1730hrs and returned at 2100hrs carrying jeeps, anti-tank guns, mortars and ammunition. The Egyptians reacted in the morning but Israeli fighters gave cover and attacked Egyptian airfields. Another Israeli paratroop lift was made on 13 November when two parachute companies dropped on an airstrip 130 miles (210km) south of the pass. They were reinforced by an infantry battalion transported by Dakotas, and Noratlases on loan from the French Air Force.

On 30 October Britain and France asked Israel to halt her advance 10 miles (16km) east of the canal, and agree to a cease-fire and to temporary occupation by the British and French of Port Said, Ismailia and Suez. Israel accepted these proposals.

Right: **An Ilyushin Il-12 military transport of the Yugoslavian Air Force. It was a multi-purpose aircraft capable of roles from glider towing, paratroop transport to cargo/passenger carrier.** *(APN)*

Left: **The Douglas C-124 Globemaster II produced for the USAF was an extensively modified version of the C-74. The wings, tail unit, engines and other well tested features of the C-74 were utilised. The double deck interior could accommodate up to 200 troops. It was also capable of carrying all types of military equipment including missiles. The aircraft shown is a C-124A with retrofitted APS-42 nose mounted radar (part C-124 C standard) and is fitted out as a troop carrier.** *(BR)*

On 31 October the RAF bombed four Egyptian airfields. Bombing, and strafing by the RAF and Fleet Air Arm, continued until the invasion was launched. By then 172 Egyptian Air Force aircraft had been destroyed: 91 out of 110 Mig–15s; 11 out of 14 Meteors; 30 out of 44 Vampires; and 26 out of 27 Il–28s.

The operation was code-named Musketeer. British and French air and land forces had been assembled on Cyprus. At dawn on 5 November their transport aircraft took off. The French, who numbered 500, were in 17 Noratlases and made their first drop on a 2,625 x 985ft (800 x 300m) area of sand beside the canal. They jumped from 490ft (150m), which was 100ft (30m) below the authorised height, without casualties except for one sergeant killed by anti-aircraft fire. Their second drop was made south of Port Said on the other side of the canal. The RAF's 18 Valettas each had 20 paratroops of the 3rd Parachute Battalion aboard, out of 600 taking part in Musketeer. Fourteen Hastings carried jeeps and anti-tank artillery as underslung loads between the undercarriage legs, which of course affected the aeroplanes' performance. Their first drop, at 0715hrs, was on El Gamil airfield two miles (3.2km) west of Port Said, another narrow strip. Sycamore and Whirlwind helicopters on HMS *Theseus* played a small part in transporting personnel.

The whole plan for the operation lacked boldness. The main assault was seaborne, no more troops were brought in by air and no use was made of El Gamil airfield.

Political dissension in Britain and widespread

Right: **A De Havilland Devon C. MkI of the Metropolitan Communications Squadron. The Royal Navy also operated the same type; the Sea Devon.** *(BR)*

Below: **Blackburn Beverley C Mk I's of No 53 Squadron RAF being loaded on a desert airfield in Aden. When used for air dropping supplied the aircrafts rear doors were removed.** *(MOD)*

international criticism of the Anglo-French invasion, resulted in the allies declaring a sudden cease-fire at 1700hrs GMT on 6 November.

Musketeer had not been a popular success, but it did make the Air Ministry and War Office aware of the fact that the Royal Air Force was dangerously ill equipped with transport aircraft. The reason for its neglect was that, being the flying Service, its paramount business was with fighters and bombers. Anything to do with hauling freight and participating in ground warfare was secondary: it always will be in the minds of most of those who serve in it, but there is now a broader-minded and more perspicacious attitude at the highest level.

Its latest type, the Blackburn Beverley, had made its first flight on 17 June 1953 and the first production aircraft first flew on 29 January 1955. The RAF bought 47 and production ceased when the last one was delivered in May 1958. When introduced it was the biggest aircraft delivered to the RAF and the first specifically designed for the dropping of heavy Army equipment through rear loading doors.

The Aircraft had four 2,850hp Bristol Centaurus 273 engines. The wingspan was 162ft (49.4m), length 99ft 5in (30.3m), height 38ft 9in (11.8m). Maximum speed was 238mph (383km/h) and maximum range 1,300 miles (2,092km). There were four in the crew and it could carry 94 troops, 70 paratroops or 45,000lb (20,412kg) of freight. However, to reduce the amount of payload that was attributable to the amount of fuel carried, it was restricted to some 600 miles (965km).

Above: **The production version of the Blackburn Beverley first flew on 29 January 1955 and a total of 47 was built for Royal Air Force Transport Command. The Beverley powered by four 2850 hp Bristol Centaurus radial engines, equipped four squadrons in the heavy freight, troop transport and tactical support role. It could carry up to 94 troops (58 in the cargo bay and 36 in the tail compartment).** *(MOD)*

Below: **Convair C-131D is the military version of Convairs 340 airliner.** *(BR)*

Wars and threats of wars have caused many troop movements by air since the Suez crisis. Now, the first sign of a conflict that might quickly spread prompts action. In the summer of 1958 civil war in Lebanon drew British and American forces to the scene. The USAF's C-130 Hercules was able to lift troops based in Germany direct to Beirut. The RAF's Beverleys and Hastings had to mount the lift from Cyprus, for lack of range.

The century entered its seventh decade with no indication of imminent political upheavals in the Mediterranean. In the Middle East, the incessant rumblings that had emanated since the end of the First World War caused no great alarm. Israeli Jews and Palestinian Moslems shared their country with deep antagonism and sporadic violence, but no immediate threat of warfare. In Africa, however, 1964 saw bloodshed threatened in the former Belgian Congo. In 1960 it had achieved independence and assumed a new name, Zaire, with a despot named Mobutu as President in title and dictator in fact; but most of the Belgian officials remained in office and the majority of those in commerce and industry also stayed on.

An anti-government force, whom the world's press described as no better than bloodthirsty bandits, had captured Stanleyville and held 1,300 Europeans and Americans hostage. These were threatened with massacre if the government army, which was advancing on the town, did not halt. The USA and Belgium carried out a joint operation to rescue them. Twelve USAF C-130s and four C-124s joined the Belgian Para-Commando Regiment at Kamina, 700 miles (1,125km) south of Stanleyville. At 0530hrs the next day 350 paratroops were dropped on the airfield two miles (3.2km) from Stanleyville, from which it was intended to fly the hostages out when rescued. Twenty minutes later the

Above: **A Boeing C-97D of the Military Air Transport Service (MATS) Pacific division.** *(BR)*

Above: **Fairchild C-119 Boxcar, a development of the earlier Fairchild C-82 Packet. First deliveries went to the USAF in December 1949 and when production ended in 1955 a total of 946 had been built. A further 141 were built for the Mutual Defense Assistance Program.** *(BR)*

rest of the airborne contingent arrived to land jeeps and more troops.

In the fighting that followed, seven Belgian paras died and the rebels murdered 60 hostages. However before noon, the insurgents were overcome and Two days later another airlift rescued a further 300 hostages from a small town 200 miles (320km) away.

This operation was remarkable for three reasons: the troops making the attack had been flown 2,500 miles (4,020km) from Europe, to meet a fleet of aircraft that had come almost twice that distance from America to carry out a combined military assault in Africa. This was a portent of the future, when a force landed by big helicopters right in the centre of a target area, instead of on an airfield outside it, would be able to achieve victory much more speedily.

In May 1978 Zaire was again in the throes of a rebellion intended to oust President Mobutu's government. A force directed by the Congolese National Liberation Front marched into Shaba, formerly Katanga, the most southern province. When they entered Kolwezi the defence collapsed and the small white population met considerable hostility and harassment. On 14 May Mobutu asked for help to rescue the Europeans, to which the USA, France and Belgium responded.

On 18 May, two battalions of Belgian Para-Commandos set out from Brussels in 10 Sabena (the Belgian national airline) aircraft and five C-130s. Parachute drops would be made from the latter; and three more were also sent, from the Republic of Mali in north-west Africa, where they had been on another task. All these reached Kamina between

the early afternoon and midnight on 19 May after refuelling. The French Foreign Legion sent 1,400 men of its 2nd Airborne Regiment, flown in five Air France 747s direct to Kinshasha. These made their first landing 15 hours before the first Belgian airlift arrived. The French used three Transall C-160s and Zairean C-130s to make their parachute attack on Kinsasha 12 hours after arrival. The Belgians made an assault landing on the Kolwezi airport in C-130s at 0630hrs on the same day, 20 May, while some of the French jumped onto two dropping zones near the town. The operation resulted in the rescue of 2,500 civilians. In May 1997 Mobutu was overthrown in a revolution and fled the country; which was renamed the Republic of the Congo.

The multiplicity of minor crises, insurrections and other calls to arms during the so-called peacetime years since 1945 are too frequent and abundant to consider individually and most are too well publicised in the news media to need specific attention. What they have shown is that when big nations decide to intervene in a war between small

Above: **Originally designed as a freight or passenger aircraft capable of heavy payload over relatively short ranges, the Bristol Type 170 was developed further to increase range and payload. The aircraft shown is a Type 170, Mk31M of the Royal Canadian Air Force others of this Mark were purchased by Royal Australian AF, Royal New Zealand AF and what was then the Royal Pakistan AF.** *(BR)*

Left: **France also produced a twin-boomed military transport the Nord 2501 Noratlas. In June 1956, a licence agreement was signed to allow the Noratlas to be built in West Germany for the Luftwaffe. Nord also supplied six to Israel.** *(BR)*

countries, as happened in the remnants of Yugoslavia, they can move fast and in large numbers by air and when they are *in situ* can monitor and police a situation from the air. Unfortunately, the men and women sent by an impartial state are often subject to great danger and used as the puppets of politicians.

It is only when a blatant act of war is committed, as when Argentina invaded the Falkland Islands and Britain was able to retaliate effectively, and Iraq attacked Kuwait, which put the West's oil supply in jeopardy, that it is worth a major nation's while to take sides actively. As NATO's membership increases, the likelihood of nations being dragged into conflicts that do not affect them directly grows accordingly.

Above: **The CASA-201 Alcotan, first flew in 1949 and served with the Spanish Air Force in many roles.** *(BR)*

Right: **Pre-flight checks being carried out on a Scottish Aviation Twin Pioneer C Mk I at an RAF base in Malaya.** *(BR)*

Below: **Prestwick (Scottish Aviation) Pioneer, STOL light transport climbs away from a jungle airstrip in Malaya.** *(MOD)*

Unfortunately, political considerations will always apply the ultimate pressure. The politicians' justification, "We have to move in to keep out X, Y or Z, with their inimical ideology" will continue to dominate. The swiftness with which action can be taken by air makes intervention ever more probable.

An army's and air force's tactical speed and flexibility are highly desirable, and the Gulf War showed that the strategic positioning of air and ground forces can now be carried out quickly on a huge scale. Disasters such as those that befell the Germans in their Russian campaign in World War Two need never happen again. Postwar military transport aircraft are limited only by the size of available landing areas. Even this has become less of a problem since aeroplanes that can carry loads of 2000 lb and more are able to land on runways 4,000ft (1219m) long, thanks to the constant advances in design. Double-decker types can carry astonishing numbers of passengers and military freight together. With the multiplying of parachute battalions and the improvement in the protective packaging for cargo, air drops can overcome most impediments.

Helicopters' improvement in performance and capacity has done more for the effectiveness of tactical warfare than any other facet of the whole inter-related and complicated science of attack and defence, as well as casualty evacuation, reconnaissance and supply.

When a military air force lacks the number of aircraft it needs, civil airlines make up the deficiency. When an airliner is hijacked, the odds are now against the terrorists.

Big, fast helicopters that have ample fuel capacity and can refuel in flight suggest themselves as the acme of attainment as a complement to the gigantic fixed-wing aircraft.

Above: **Standard medium range transport of Soviet armed forces, the Ilyushin Il 14 was built in vast numbers. Powered by two Ash-82T 14-cylinder radial engine (developed by Shvetsov from the Pratt & Whitney Twin Wasp) the Il-14 was also built by Avia in Czechoslovakia.** *(BR)*

CHAPTER NINE

Clandestine Operations

During World War Two, spies, supplies and special forces were delivered by air into enemy territory. Operations of this type still continue.

The last day of the Allied evacuation of France in June 1940 was also the first day in the history of the French Resistance organisation. The official figure for the number of men shipped from Dunkirk is 338,226, of whom 112,000 were French. In the next two weeks 144,171 British, 18,246 French, 24,352 Poles, 4,938 Czechs and a few Belgians followed. Of the thousands who were left behind, almost all spent the rest of the war in prison camps. Of the comparatively few British who evaded capture, most strove to find a way back to Britain. Those who did not know French had to trust in the natives to help them or at least not to betray them to the enemy.

Some of the French population, either unaware of or ignoring the Fascist sympathy that was rife among the officers of their armed forces, were in any case hostile to the British, whom they blamed for the defeat. Many, however, bravely sheltered British servicemen and helped them to escape from France. Those who showed this spirit were the nucleus of a resistance organisation that soon covered the whole country. As the war progressed, however, and the countries in Europe that had fallen to Germany became increasingly aware of their dependence on Britain (and later the USA) for their future liberty, the French became as cordial as the Belgians, Dutch, Norwegians and Danes had always been. Despite their mutual antipathies, the French began to acknowledge that Britain and France as allies had beaten Germany in the Great War only 21 years before Hitler began this second one.

On the fall of France in 1940 wireless communication between London and the French resisters was quickly established. Most importantly for the RAF, a transport operation that was one of the most useful innovations the war would see was born. In the First World War, spies had often been landed behind enemy lines by both the British and French air forces. In the Second it was possible to fly them deep into any enemy-occupied country and bring them back to report what they had learned or done.

Clandestine air traffic between Britain and France was begun on the night of 19/20 October 1940 when Flight Lieutenant W. R. Farley, commanding No 419 Flight, fetched Pilot Officer Philip Schneider, whose code name was "Felix J", to England in a Lysander. Schneider, who was of Anglo-French birth and had chosen British nationality, had been parachuted into France from a Whitley ten days before. This initial pick-up was a fine feat of airmanship. The weather was atrocious. Before take-off, a bullet hit the compass and Farley had to map-read by moonlight until cloud compelled him to climb to 16,000ft (4,877m) and grope his way with a gale from the south-west blowing him off course. The petrol tank ran dry as they arrived over an unidentifiable coast that might have been in enemy hands, but when, at 0655hrs, they crash landed, proved to be the east coast of Scotland.

Flights that demanded the same expertise and courage were maintained throughout the German occupation. Most of the men and women trained

in England as wireless operators, saboteurs or organisers of Resistance groups were flown to France in Lysanders, which needed only a very short take-off and landing run, so could nip in and out of small fields. Two, sometimes three, passengers could travel in the rear cockpit. Some had to land by parachute from a Whitley, Halifax or Stirling, either because there was no suitable landing ground in the area or the enemy were so numerous and alert that the risk of attempting a landing and take-off would be too great.

Often the passengers whom the Lysanders took to England were French or British members of the Resistance going on a short rest, or to make reports and plan operations. On some nights when more than two people had to be fetched from the same place, two Lysanders were sent. French political leaders or members of the Intelligence service would be ferried over the Channel for conferences. Hudsons, which needed half a mile (0.8km) for take-off and landing, were used when several passengers had to be carried. The four-engined aircraft were also used to drop people and munitions into other enemy-occupied countries. This was done at 500 or 600ft (152 to 183m), to minimise the risk of parachutes being scattered widely.

Tempsford was the main base for the squadrons that flew on clandestine missions. Some flights were made from Tangmere. One of the Halifax squadrons, No 644 stationed at Tarrant Rushton, was ostensibly training to tow gliders while also making secret sorties for the Special Operations Executive, which

ran all the British intelligence and other secret activities. Flight Sergeant (later Warrant Officer) Alan Matthews, who was a navigator in the squadron, says "Bomber crews often couldn't find their targets, but we had to be able to find a specific field".

His pilot was Flight Lieutenant R. F. W. Cleaver DSO. On 5 April 1944 the crew were briefed to drop arms and ammunition to a Resistance group in the southern part of Charente Maritime. They took off at 2226hrs and, to ensure accurate navigation, flew at 2,000ft (610m). The ceiling for light Flak (20mm) was 6,500ft (1,980m). When they arrived over the dropping zone there was no signal light from the ground, so they had to abort the sortie. Their homeward track crossed the defended area around Cognac airfield at 1,500ft (457m). Anti-aircraft fire set their starboard inner engine on fire, stopped the starboard outer and set the wing alight. Cleaver ordered his crew to bale out and Alan Matthews, who could not swim, descended into the Charente river. Thanks to his life jacket, he managed to scramble out, knocked on the door of the first house he came to and was invited in. The penalty for harbouring a British subject was death. This did not daunt his benefactor. Flight Sergeant Matthews spent the next six months as a machine gunner in the Fougre Maquis and was finally taken home in a Hudson.

Richard Cleaver forced-landed the burning Halifax, which was carrying ammunition and explosives, in a field. He got out before the whole cargo detonated, evaded capture, reached Gibraltar

Above: **Entering RAF service in 1938 with No 16 Squadron as a two-seat army cooperation aircraft, the remarkable STOL handling characteristics of the Westland Lysander allowed it to perform many tasks. The aircraft shown is a Lysander III SCW (fitted with a belly-mounted auxiliary fuel tank) and was used to deliver and collect special passengers or agents from mainly occupied France.** *(HC)*

and arrived back in England on 22 June. In August he was awarded the DFC.

A totally different sort of clandestine transport operation, one of the most audacious feats and most brilliant displays of flying, was triumphantly executed in December 1944. The aeroplane involved was the most versatile light aircraft in the world and the smallest transport type, the Fieseler Storch (stork). This had made its maiden flight in May 1936 and was delivered to the Luftwaffe a year later. With a wingspan of 46ft 9in (14.25m) and length 32ft 6in (9.9m), powered by a 240hp Argus As 10C engine, its top speed was 109mph (175km/h). Its take-off run was only 213ft (65m) and it needed only 66ft (20m) for landing. A 7.92mm MG15 machine gun could be mounted at the upper rear of the cabin. It was unique in the world: of substantial size, with room for three passengers, more power than most light aeroplanes had and with a breathtaking STOL capability. General-leutnant Ernst Udet who, as well as being a Great War fighter ace was an exceptional pilot, actually hovered the prototype against a light wind in 1936. The Luftwaffe used it as a conveyance for senior staff officers, general communications and casualty evacuation.

It was Benito Mussolini, the Italian dictator, who was the reason for the Storch's most dramatic and dangerous escapade. On 25 July 1943 Vittorio Emanuele, King of Italy, found the courage to dismiss him and appoint Marshal Badoglio to form a new government. Mussolini was immediately arrested and whisked off to internment in a place of which

Below: **Westland Lysander I over Beirut, Lebanon.** *(BR)*

the Germans did not know; and from which, if they did find out, should not be able to liberate him. The intention was to hand him over to the Allies as soon as they ratified the peace treaty for which Italy had asked and was keeping secret.

News of Mussolini's dismissal and disappearance reached the Germans at once and a hunt for him began. They were baffled, but there was to be a *deus*

ex machina to solve their dilemma, a Viennese, Leutnant Otto Skorzeny. He was not a professional soldier. Born in 1908, he was a partner in a building firm. On the outbreak of war he volunteered for the Luftwaffe, was turned down as too old and conscripted into the artillery of the Waffen S. S. He fought in the Russian campaign with distinction and was invalided home in December 1942, medically

classified as fit for home service only. He was no Nazi, but inactivity was unbearable for a man of his vigour and intelligence and whatever he undertook he did with great enthusiasm.

Hitler had belatedly ordered the creation of a Commando unit. Like Churchill's directive nearly three years previously, it was ill received by the General Staff. Also, like Churchill, Hitler had to be

Above: **Troops loading a standard supply container in the Western Desert, October 1942.** *(BR)*

Above: **A captured Fiesler Storch in Allied invasion markings.** *(BR)*

officer would be no threat to them, as would be a career officer if he managed to make a success of the job. On 20 April 1943 Otto Skorzeny was gazetted Chief of Germany's Special Troops. Carl Radl became his adjutant and settled down to study reports of British raids. Skorzeny founded a Commando school. He knew that the RAF dropped and picked up spies in occupied Europe, so he went to Holland to interview Resistance members who had been captured and turned double-agent. All the proposals for raids that he made were rejected by the General Staff, to whom, like all their kind, any unorthodoxy was anathema. But, when Mussolini's disappearance became known, Skorzeny was summoned to Hitler's Headquarters, told to rescue Mussolini and was introduced to his new chief, the jovial General Kurt Student, Commander of the Airborne Force, and his personal pilot, Hauptmann Gerlach, another brilliant flyer.

obeyed (even more so: the British Prime Minister did not have openly dissenting senior officers shot!). Fortuitously, Skorzeny's great friend Carl Radl, a lawyer in civilian life, was a minor staff officer and in a position to put forward his name. The Generals accepted it willingly. An unknown temporary junior

First, Skorzeny had to find Mussolini. There were many rumours about his whereabouts and reported sightings of him on Ponza, a small island 120 miles

Above: **With leading edge slats and full-span flaps extended the Fiesler Fi-156 Storch could almost 'hover' when landing into a moderate wind.** *(BR)*

Left: **The Fiesler Fi-156 Storch first flew early in 1936 and entered service with the Luftwaffe in 1937. Powered by a 240hp Argus AS-10c it was also built in occupied France by Morane Saulnier. That same company continued production of F-156 after 1945.** *(BR)*

Right: **The Chase XC-123 first flew on 14 October 1949, but Chase did not build any of the 300 ordered. Fairchild won the production contract designing and constructing all future variants. The aircraft shown is an early Fairchild built C-123B Provider.** *(BR)*

Below: **De Havilland of Canada designed and built the DHC-4 Caribou as a STOL transport. It was ordered by the RCAF as a CC-108 and later by the US Army as the CV-2 (later C-7).** *(BR)*

(193km) west of Naples, then in Spezia, next to the island of Maddalena off the north-east coast of Sardinia. Here he found that Mussolini was indeed being held in a strongly guarded villa. Soon after, word came of Mussolini's presence on another small island, off Elba. More false leads followed until an intercepted signal in code revealed the truth.

Mussolini had been moved to the Gran Sasso, at 10,000ft (3,050m) the highest mountain in Italy. Newly built, the Hotel Campo Imperatore at 6,000ft (1,830m) was the only place where he could be. The sole access to it was by a funicular. All the roads leading to the Gran Sasso had been closed. Skorzeny and Radl were flown over the mountain to take photographs. The massive building stood on a spur, with a triangular ledge in front of it. The whole area at the base of the mountain was swarming with troops and Carabinieri and 250 were reported to be in the hotel. Merely to cut the mountain off would need a division, let alone assaulting it.

The triangular plot of ground held Skorzeny's attention as a possible landing ground for gliders – not many, though. He calculated the time it would take to pull off such a difficult *coup de main*. How long would it take the surprised Italian guards to get Mussolini to the funicular? Would they shoot him rather than let him be captured?

He put a plan to Student and two of his staff. They did not think much of it, but there seemed no alternative. It would be impossible to drop

Above: **Royal Air Force Transport Command operated 20 Bristol type 175 Britannia's as long range all-purpose transports. Designated C.MkI all were 253 series aircraft powered by four 4445ehp Bristol Siddeley Proteus 765 turboprop engines. The RAF also operated three 252 series Britannia's as C.Mk2.** *(MOD)*

Right: **Douglas C-133 Cargomaster about to be loaded.** *(BR)*

Below: **First flown on 23 August 1954 the Lockheed C-130 Hercules remains in production in 1998** *(BR)*

paratroops: at that altitude, they would hurtle down at such speed that they would burst like rotten pomegranates when they hit the mountain ledge. The only feasible means of abducting Mussolini was to send his paratroops in to sieze the lower funicular station and land gliders on the mountain ledge. They must expect heavy casualties. When Skorzeny explained the plan to his troops they all volunteered. Another party of them would capture Aquila airfield, a few miles away. He would rush their captive there and a waiting aircraft would fly them to Rome. In case something went wrong, a Storch was to land in the valley and fly Mussolini and Skorzeny out.

Left: **Whitworth Gloster AW.660 Argosy medium range military transport entered RAF service, as the C.Mk I, in March 1962. A total of 56 were ordered and were powered by four Rolls-Royce Dart RDa.8, Mk 101 turboprop engines.** *(BR)*

The paratroops who would capture the funicular station were to drop at dawn, but the gliders were being towed from the south of France and did not arrive until 1100 hrs. They could not postpone the operation for fear that any delay could ruin it. Dropping late in the day would mean warm air currents among the mountains that might wreck the gliders. The benefit of a late start was that nobody would be expecting a raid in broad daylight.

Twelve aeroplanes and their gliders took off at 1300hrs. Reluctantly in the leading glider with Skorzeny was a pro-German Italian General, Soletti, whose presence Radl hoped would have an adverse psychological effect on the defenders. Unknown to

Above: **US Navy Grumman Trader on board HMS Ark Royal 14 October 1957.** *(BR)*

Skorzeny, two aircraft fell into bomb craters on their take-off runs. When, at 12000ft (3,660m), his glider and tug broke cloud, he saw that the two leading couples were not in sight. He told his glider pilot to drop the tow and as they began to descend they saw that the surface of the triangle where they hoped to land was not level; it sloped towards the mountainside and the surface was rough with rocky bumps. One of Student's orders was that if they could not make a smooth landing they must

abandon the attack and go down to the bottom of the valley. Skorzeny disobeyed. The crash landing shattered the glider. He led his few men in storming the hotel. The defenders were too surprised and too confused by the sight of an Italian general to shoot. Upstairs, Skorzeny confronted Mussolini and two Italian officers, whom two German soldiers dragged away. Four gliders came swooping down and slammed on to the landing area. The occupants of one, dead or injured, did not emerge but the troops

Below: **A later version of the Lockheed Hercules. This C-130E was one of four supplied to the Iranian Air Force.** *(JM)*

Right: **Two STOL utility transports built by De Havilland Canada and supplied to US forces. The upper aircraft is a U-6A Beaver, the lower a U-1 Otter.** *(BR)*

178

in the other three stormed the building. Skorzeny summoned the garrison's commanding officer, a colonel, and demanded his surrender.

A telephone call from the lower funicular station reported that it was in the paratroops' hands. The radio failed to make contact with Rome; and the Storch waiting in the valley had damaged its landing gear. But Gerlach was there, orbiting the hotel in his Storch. The troops, both German and Italian, moved the biggest boulders from the ledge and

Gerlach landed. When Skorzeny told him that he would have to fly him out with the prisoner aboard, he refused. Skorzeny reminded him that this would be a deliberate refusal to obey Hitler's order that Mussolini must be brought out whatever it took. The only possible consequence for them would be to honour the German officers' code and blow their brains out. Gerlach changed his mind.

In order to make the probably impossible take-off, a grotesque expedient had to be resorted to. When they boarded the aeroplane, 12 men took hold of a rope tied to its tail and restrained it while the engine was run up to take-off revolutions. When Gerlach gave a signal they dropped the rope and he opened the throttle to full bore. The lurching machine shot off the brink of the ledge, buckling a wheel in the process, and dived steeply into the valley. A few hundred feet from the bottom, Gerlach levelled off and flew to Rome. Hitler telephoned his delighted congratulations and awarded Skorzeny an immediate Knight's Cross.

Above: **Beagle Aircraft Limited built 20 of the B206 series 1 (B.206R) Beagle for the RAF. These were operated as the CC.Mk I Basset for communications and ferrying personnel, including V-Bomber crews.** *(BR)*

Below: **Shorts Skyvan series 3M, light military STOL transport.** *(APN)*

Post-War Clandestine Operations

Below: **The RAF operated eight De Havilland Comet C.Mk 2's as long range mixed passenger and cargo transports. In 1962 the RAF took delivery of the first of five Comet C.Mk 4's and all were standard civilian 4C aircraft.** *(BR)*

The heirs of the Flying Tigers, officially and successively known as the American Volunteer Group and the China Air Task Force, were reactivated after the Second World War as Air America (AA). Under this guise the force was formed and run by the Central Intelligence Agency (CIA), a fact that was remarkable in view of the CIA's dedication to secrecy, for the flamboyance of the characters it attracted was bound to incite curiosity; but security was at least baffling enough to ensure that nobody knew exactly what Air America did.

Its pilots were of the same breed as those who had earned the title Flying Tigers: hard-drinking, piratical, unconventional and combat toughened.

The conclusions drawn from their appearance and manner by those who knew nothing about their duties was misleading. They were not mere unreliable adventurers, they were men of immense courage, skill and with many thousands of hours in the air, they flew superbly. As the famous James "Ginger" Lacey, the RAF's top-scoring pilot in the Battle of Britain, said, "It's always the best pilots who get into trouble". In other words, a streak of recklessness – correctly applied – is what lifts them above the average.

The activities of AA were so diverse that some of them defy credulity; but all are supported by hard evidence. It was a crypto-military outfit whose attitude was totally ruthless: whatever needed to be done had to be done. Among its covert actions was a parachute drop of Tibetan horsemen to fight a guerrilla war in the Himalayas; supplying rice to

Left: **Although painted in Aeroflot colours this is a military version (note rear gun turret) of the Il;yushin Il-76. First flown on 25 March 1977 the Il-76 was powered by four Soloviev D-30KP turbofans.** *(JM)*

Left: **Only ten Short Belfast C.Mk I heavy transports were built for the RAF Air Support Command. Capable of carrying up to 200 troops it was powered by four Rolls-Royce Tyne RTy.12 engines.** *(BR)*

30,000 opium farmers and flying their produce to market; dropping ammunition to mercenaries and other guerrilla fighters. All these missions were instigated by the CIA.

The AA pilots were dedicated to the service of their country and the fight against the spread of Communism. Also under CIA direction, they operated extensively over China. They supplied besieged Nationalist towns with food and medical aid, they delivered metals to armament factories and even cash to impoverished banks to help sustain the economy of impoverished states co-operating in CIA activities. The terrain over which they flew was wild and they had neither accurate weather forecasts nor reliable wireless communications.

Air America began its activities in 1948, with some of the most experienced pilots in the world flying C-46s and C-47s. In time they were equipped with jets; and when helicopter range and capacity

Left: **Fourteen BAC (Vickers Armstrong) model 1106, VC-10 transports were ordered for the Royal Air Force. Later all were modified to air tankers when HP Victors were retired from service.** *(BR)*

Above: **A Boeing C-135 Stratolifter developed from the Model 367-80.** *(JM)*

Right: **One of four NAMC YS-11's operated by the Japan's Air Self-Defence Force.** *(JM)*

made it worthwhile, these were added to the stable and the best pilots who had made their reputations in Vietnam were gathered in. All of them – fixed or rotary-wing jocks – operated everywhere in the Far East. They carried freight, often of a kind that would give a Customs official or pacifist a fit, or small espionage teams to remote areas at night in helicopters, to be landed, or by aeroplane to drop by parachute; and fetched back to base when their furtive assignments were completed.

Despite information obtainable now by satellites, there will always be a need for men to garner intelligence on the spot and they will be taken there and recovered by the most suitable aircraft.

The Falklands and Gulf Wars

At 0430hrs on 2 April 1982, 150 troops of the Argentinian Special Forces landed by helicopter at Mullet Creek, three miles (4.8km) south-west of Port Stanley in the Falkland Islands. Their vernacular title was "Buzo Tactico". In Castilian Spanish the first word is slang for "alert" and the second means "tactician". Both, judging by the subsequent performance of the invading troops, were ill applied. At 0930hrs 1,000 more special troops and Marines landed. They were ferried in a series of return journeys by a pair of Lockheed C-130K Hercules,

Above: **Antonov An-26, NATO code name: Curl, short-range transport.** *(JM)*

Above: **The An-12 was the cargo version of the Antonov An-10 and featured a completely re-designed rear fuselage, featuring a loading ramp. The An-12, NATO code name Cub, was powered by four Ivchenko AI-20K turboprops.**
(JM)

of the eight that the Argentinian Air Force owned. The AAF's two Victors refuelled them in flight. The grossly outnumbered Port Stanley garrison of 80 British troops had to surrender.

The Argentians also flew a variety of helicopters – Pumas and Bell 212H-83s, Skyvans and a Beaver floatplane. Between the invasion and the surrender on 14 June, they made only 14 sorties to the islands to deliver 304 troops and 70 tonnes of freight.

Shortly before the British ground force began a counter-attack, Argentina impressed all civil registered aircraft and gave their crews temporary ranks. Among these aeroplanes were seven Learjets,

an HS 125-700B, six Aero Commandos and seven Eurostars. The British airlifts in support of its recapture of the Falklands, over 12,000 miles (19,200km) from Britain, were via Ascenscion Island, flown by the Hercules and VC10.

The logistics for the Gulf War show a far greater scale of movement.

Two routes for strategic airlift were in operation: Desert Express and European Desert Express. In late October the (USAF) Military Airlift Command announced a special airlift operation named Desert Express to provide daily air delivery of spare parts considered absolutely crucial to the war effort. This

Right: **Aeritalia (originally Fiat) G-222 multi-purpose military transport. First flown in summer 1970 the G-222 is powered by two Fiat built General Electric T64-GE-P4D turboprops.**
(JM)

Above: **Two VC-10's of the RAF. The lead aircraft is a dedicated tanker aircraft whilst the aircraft being refuelled is a duel purpose tanker/transport aircraft. All the RAF's VC-10 transports were eventually converted to tankers, replacing Victors, by Flight Refuelling Limited.** *(CC)*

Left: **A Lockheed C-130 Hercules, known affectionately to the crews who fly it as the 'Charlie One Thirty', banks away from the camera ship.** *(Lockheed)*

Right: **The Lockheed C-130H is similar to earlier models of the Hercules but has an improved wing, more powerful engines (four Allison T56-A-15 turboprops) and up to date avionics. A 'new' Hercules, C-130J, is under development.** *(Lockheed)*

Below: **Pre-flight checks in the cockpit of a Lockheed C-130H Hercules. The multiple windowed cockpit affords the 130's crew excellent vision.** *(Lockheed)*

Left: **A Lockheed C-130 Hercules in service with the RAF drops a special load pannier. The aircraft is flown low and slow across the field. The load is then pulled from the aircraft by a parachute to land with a 'thump' but with no damage to the load.** *(Lockheed)*

Right: **A Grumman VC-11A Gulfstream II, powered by two Rolls-Royce Spey turbofans, in service with the US Coastguard as a VIP transport.**
(JM)

Left: **Derived from the E-2A Hawkeye the Grumman C-2A Greyhound is a carrier on-board delivery (COD) transport. Many of the C-2's components are compatible with those of the E-2. The aircraft is capable of catapult launches and arrested landings. It can carry up to 28 passengers. has a crew of two and is powered by two Alison T56-A-425 turboprops.** *(JM)*

Below: **Designed to meet the specific requirements of West German and French Forces the Transall (Transport Allianz) C-160 first flew on 9 April 1981. The Transall replaced Fairchild C-119s and Nord Noratlas aircraft in service with both countries forces.** *(JM)*

Above: **Flown for the first time 30 June 1968 the Lockheed C-SA Galaxy was designed to meet specification CX-HLS (Cargo, Experimental-Heavy Logistics System). In 1978 a contract was issued to Lockheed for the replacement of C-5 wings, which were virtually a new design. The C-5B was given production approval in 1982.** *(Lockheed)*

Above: **The nose section of the Lockheed C-5 Galaxy lifts up to facilitate rapid loading.**
(Lockheed)

Left: **Powered by four 41,000 lb thrust General Electric TF39-GE-1C turbofans, a Lockheed C-5 Galaxy takes-off on another mission.**
(Lockheed)

Right: **Purchased from British Airways in 1982 by the RAF to fulfil an urgent requirement for passenger/tanker aircraft, Lockheed L1011-50 TriStars were converted as TriStar K Mk I.**

Below: **McDonnell Douglas DC-9-30 in military service as C-9 Nightingale replacing Convair C-131's.** *(JM)*

was a new concept of airlift operations that involved regular scheduled, dedicated aircraft for daily delivery. European Desert Express was a similar operation that originated in Europe rather than the continental United States. Aircraft departed Ramstein and picked up cargo at Rhein Main Air Base once daily, seven days a week.

The bulk of the military strategic airlift was carried by USAF C-5 and C-141 transports. The numbers in the table reflect airlift "missions" rather than "sorties", the term most often used in this report for aircraft operations. In airlift parlance, the term sortie is related to the aircraft and refers to a

take-off, flight and landing; a C-141 making the trip Charleston – Lajes – Rhein Main – Cairo – Dharan would have made four sorties. The term mission, however, is related to the final destination of the cargo, and how many missions are logged was determined by the cargo status. The C-141 that left Charleston with the cargo for Dharan, and made several intermediate stops to refuel, pick up passengers, etc., still completed only one mission. Mission totals are used as the unit of measure in accordance with the airlift system's reporting conventions because the intent of this table is to reflect the movement of cargo to a final destination.

Above: **Designed to replace the JASDF ageing fleet of C-46 Commando's the Kawasaki C-1 is a medium range transport. The two pylon-mounted engines are Mitsubishi (Pratt & Whitney) JT8D-M-9 turbofans.** *(BR)*

Left: **A Piaggio P.166-DL3 is a turboprop powered (two Avco Lycoming LP101-600) multi-purpose light transport. It can carry ten paratroops, or can operate as a light tactical transport amongst its many roles.** *(BR)*

Far left: **Lockheed C-130 Hercules of the RAF. The aircraft is a C Mk 1P, equipped for in-flight refuelling.**

Right **Lockheed's Model 1329 Jetstar, a four jet engined utility transport, was used by the USAF Communications Service, as the C-140A, to inspect world wide military navigation aids. The VC-140A was used as a VIP transport by Military Airlift Command.** *(BR)*

Right: **De Havilland DHC-6 Twin Otter saw service with RCAF as the CC-138, the US Army and USAF as the UV-18B, plus many more smaller air forces throughout the world. A true STOL performer the Twin Otter can also be equipped with floats or skis.** *(JM)*

Below: **Airtec CN-235 was a joint design project between CASA of Spain and Nortanio of Indonesia. Shown is the CN-235M military transport.** *(BR)*

Above: **Lockheed C-141 Starlifter in formation with a C-130 Hercules.**
(Lockheed)

Left: **US Air Force technicians carry out systems checks in the cockpit of a Lockheed C-141 Starlifter.**
(Lockheed)

Data extracted from the situation reports for Desert Shield. Given below is the official summary of the airlift from August 1990 to March 1991.

The aircraft concerned were C-141 DS/DS, C-141 DE, C-141 EE, C-141, C-5, KC-10 and unspecified civilian types.

Total Missions 16,090.
Total short tons (tonnes) 538,840.
Total passengers 499,627."

CHAPTER TEN

The Future

Air forces are now able not only to deliver fire power directly by employing air-to-air and air-to-surface weapons, but also by airlifting combat units at high speed over great distances.

In considering the size, equipment and performance of future military transport aircraft, it should be remembered that in the history of heavier-than-air flight they are comparative newcomers. Even in the period during which aircraft have been designed for war, the transport type is a neophyte. The progress made might seem slow, but to have progressed as far as it has in a comparatively short time is impressive. Samuel Johnson said of a dog walking on its hind legs, "It is not done well, but you are surprised to find it done at all". In the subject under review here, such a comparison would be ungracious but apt.

The use of air power in the form of heavier than-air aircraft as an instrument of war is still, historically, in its infancy. However, air forces are now able not only to deliver fire power directly by employing air-to-air and air-to-surface weapons, but also by airlifting combat units at high speed over great distances.

As the means of delivering troops and equipment to a battle area, air transport has replaced sea power; but it is not long since the former was the only means available. The Arab–Israeli War in 1973 was over by the time the first seaborne supplies from the USA arrived in Israel. While a ship was making best speed across the Atlantic and Mediterranean, the USAF and Israeli military and civil aeroplanes had flown 27,000 tonnes to Israel; and the USSR had air lifted 15,000 tonnes of war materiel to Egypt and Syria.

Aircraft designed to carry troops and equipment over the long distances covered by the movement of a strategic force must satisfy at least the following basic demands: 1. The ability to carry personnel and/or cargo; 2. A cruising speed of at least Mach 0.75; 3. A large payload in weight and size, carrying a wide variety of military hardware e.g. artillery, armoured personnel carriers, trucks and small helicopters: 4. A range of at least 2,500 n.m. with maximum payload; 5. Rapid on-load and off-load, which need large cargo doors and integral ramps for wheeled and tracked vehicles.

It is imperative to have as many of these features as possible, especially for the aircraft to be able to fly combined strategic and tactical missions such as a trans-ocean flight followed by an air drop, or by a landing on airfields that have not been fully prepared for them.

In general, design has featured a high wing with lift-enhancing devices, an elevated tail, low-slung fuselage and high flotation landing gear (a combination of suspension, wheels and tyres that can absorb severe stresses on take-off and landing). These are necessary for operations from unpaved airfields and to provide a big cargo compartment that can be quickly loaded and unloaded through an integral ramp and big rear doors.

Such objectives are more easily achieved now than in the past and will become increasingly feasible, thanks to increasingly durable materials, high-lift systems and more efficient engines.

Air transportation plays an increasingly important part in the exercising of military and political power by performing a great variety of tasks. Many areas

around the globe, such as Central America, Southern Africa, the Arabian Gulf and the whole Middle East, are in an almost constant state of conflict. The Third World is unstable and expected to remain so for many years. The outlook is for threats emanating from several directions and lack of the infrastructure necessary for rapid movement. Large standing armies are not only a heavy economic burden on the state but also a potential destabilising factor.

In the West, airlift forces are expected to become increasingly significant for other reasons. Demographic, economic and political considerations will put democratic nations under increasing pressure to reduce the size of their land, sea and air forces. If such demands prevail, the ability to deploy the reduced armed forces quickly wherever they are needed will be more critical than ever. No country's air transport forces can yet cope with the maximum demands made of them, as the high proportion of civil aircraft used in the Gulf War has shown.

The most important attribute in a transport aircraft is its capacity to carry the very largest items of military equipment. The C-130, C-160 and AN-22 can accommodate what are known as "oversize" loads. This term applies to tractors weighing as much as 40,000lb, self-propelled artillery, armoured fighting vehicles, helicopters (dismantled), bulldozers, bridge-laying equipment and main battle tanks that weigh up to 120,000lb. Such loads have been carried by the C-5, AN-14 and AN-22. The outsize loads are of prime importance because they give a combat force the ability to fight with maximum effect.

There are not enough airfields in the world capable of accepting the larger airlift aircraft. This sometimes necessitates a big aeroplane landing at a big field and transferring its load to smaller aeroplanes. That is wasteful of time and money, necessitates duplication of cargo-handling equipment, and can cause congestion at the smaller aerodromes, which makes enemy interdiction easier.

In addition to the general and obvious need for designers and constructors to be striving constantly to improve the all-round ability of their products and develop systems that require as little maintenance as possible, those engaged in producing military transports have to think about equipping them with radar warning sensors, missile jammers and chaff dispensers.

It is manifest that the great variations in countries' defence policies make it impossible to arrive at a universal concept of air transport operations. Many nations are increasing the proportion of their ground forces that can be deployed by air, which follows the trend in general mobility and means that the demand for airlifting will grow. In consequence, manufacturers must expect to be required to develop aircraft that will be able to land on 3,000ft airfields. The benefits of this requirement will be to ease congestion at major airfields, overcome the inefficiencies of transloading, and, most important, enable loads to be delivered as quickly and as close as possible to where they are needed. Flexibility and all-round efficiency will benefit.

The critera for future aircraft are: 1. The size,

Above: **The massive Antonov An-225, Mriya (Dream) carrying the Soviet space shuttle Buran (Snowstorm). Crewed by six personnel including two flight engineers the An-225 powered by six 51590lb thrust Lotarev D-18T turbofans, was the first aircraft to be flown at a gross weight of over one million pounds. To support its massive weight the Mriya is fitted with two, twin-wheel nose units and seven-each side, twin-wheel main units.** *(JM)*

weight and amount of equipment to be carried; 2. Inter-theatre distances; 3. Locations of airfields likely to be used; 4. Airfield dimensions, including taxiways and parking ramps as well as runways; 5. Ground manoeuvrability; 6. Reliability.

The Aircraft must be able to carry maximum payload from a runway not more than 8,000ft over a minimum distance of 2,400 n.m. It must also be able to cary loads such as main battle tanks into forward airfields with runways of 3,000 to 4,000ft. This means low take-off and landing speeds, short take-off and landing runs and ability to touch down with great precision at the required point. This can be done by using "powered lift", i.e. directing the engine efflux onto and through large double-slotted flaps to increase the coefficient of lift on the supercritical wings.

The requirement is to be met by a thrust-reverser that can be selected in flight immediately before touchdown. Instead of engine efflux being emitted forward, down and to the sides, stirring up dust, reverse thrust deflected forward and upward can be safely selected at any speed, on any surface: thus the sudden restoration of forward power towards the end of a landing run stirring up debris and doing engine damage is avoided.

An important feature at airfields is the capacity of parking ramps. The USAF has specified that

Below: **The STOL Antonov An-72 is a light transport for military and civil use powered by two Lotarev D-36 high by-pass ratio turbofans. Equipped as an all-weather aircraft it can also be equipped with ski landing gear for operation of snow and ice.** *(BR)*

aircraft must be able to complete a 180 degree turn within a 90ft wide runway. At airfields with parallel runways or turnaround loops at the ends they must be able to use 60ft wide runways. Off loading while engines are running obviously reduces turn round time but can be dangerous to ground staff as even at ground-idling speed dust and debris might be blown around. Deflecting the efflux up at 30 degrees avoids this.

It is essential that the whole hold be utilised and cargo carried on the ramp, which must have the same load-bearing capacity. Maximum payload capacity is made possible by the use of titanium and advanced composite structures to lighten weight, and the hold needs to take large vehicles in double rows. Paratroops can be carried and a low altitude parachute extraction system enables heavy loads to be landed with great precision.

The current vexed question is about the Future Large Aircraft, about which a decision is so long overdue that the countries that are awaiting it are likely to abandon the project and settle for a suitable aeroplane that is already available.

In the early 1980s the need was first recognised that in about the year 2000 the Hercules and Transall would need to be replaced. Three European companies, ACrospatiale, British Aerospace and MBB joined forces with Lockheed as the Future International Military Airlifter (FIMA) consortium. In 1987 they were joined by Alenia and CASA. The

consortium's purpose was to examine the possibility of meeting NATO needs by a common aircraft design. In 1985 Defence Ministries of the Independent European Programme (IEPG) instructed their National Armament Directors to begin examining ways of meeting their future needs to replace transport, tanker, maritime and similar sized aircraft by developing and producing in collaboration a single, basic, common aircraft. Such a solution, if possible, would have economic and operational benefits for European and NATO air forces. Thus was born the Future Large Aircraft (FLA) project.

In 1989 six European air forces were near to reaching agreement on an Outline European Staff Target (OEST). It then became apparent that to have an American company in the industrial consortium would be a complication as there was "no USA military involvement on the Government side". Moreover, Lockheed evidently wished to pursue its own interests, which no longer seemed to fit the consortium's engagement to European industry in the development of a successor to the Hercules. This led to a decision to disband FIMA and five European countries formed Euroflag, the European Future Large Aircraft Group. In 1991 Euroflag formed a joint venture company, Euroflag SrI, in Rome. Its role was to co-ordinate and manage industry's involvement in the FLA programme and to fulfil the responsibilities of prime contractor. The co-

Above: **The Soviet equivalent to the Lockheed C-5 Galaxy is the Antonov An-124 Ruslan (a giant hero of Russian folklore). In 1985 an An-124 set a payload (377,473 lb) to height (35,269 ft) record beating the previous one, by 53 per cent, achieved by a C-5 Galaxy.** *(JM)*

Above: **Boeing VC-25A 'Air Force One' one of two 747-200's converted for US Presidential transports. Boeing also modified 19 ex-PanAm 747's for the Civil Reserve Air Fleet (CRAF) program under the USAF designation C-19A.** *(BR)*

Below: **A McDonnell Douglas KC-10A Extender.** *(HG)*

equal shareholders, Aerospatiale, Alenia, British Aerospace, CASA and Deutsche Aerospace give technical and commercial support to this company. The main partners in Airbus Industries are all co-equal shareholders in Euroflag, so bring to the FLA long experience in collaboration and the modern technology of the successful Airbus project, with the experince of other national and collaborative military projects.

In late 1991 the air forces of Belgium, France, Germany, Italy, Portugal, Spain and Turkey signed the FLA Outline European Staff Target, after agreeing on harmonised operational requirements. In 1992 the five European SrI companies and FLABE 1 of Belgium, OGMA of Portugal and TAI of Turkey did 12 months of pre-feasibility studies managed by Euroflag SrI. In December 1992 a comprehensive joint report was issued.

Seven European air forces were close to agreeing on a very detailed set of harmonised requirements

Left: **'Air Force One' of 1962 was a converted Boeing 707-353B for Presidential duties. It was flown as a VC-137C by the 89th Military Airlift Wing based at Andrews AFB, Maryland.** *(BR)*

set out in a European Staff Target (EST). FLA was about to enter the feasibility stage. Euroflag was discussing the final details of an 18-month feasibility study to be funded by Governments. BAE was to fund its own workshare as it did in the pre-feasibility phase and the study would begin later that year.

In March 1993 an international symposium was held at Strasbourg to discuss the future importance of military aircraft not only in war but also in providing emergency relief by landing or dropping supplies after disasters such as earthquakes, volcanic eruptions, floods and famine. Transport aeroplanes and/or helicopters are often the only means of giving assistance.

The end of the East/West confrontation initiated a reduction in the size of armed forces under both political and public pressure to reduce defence spending. The Western Union Nations have recognised the need to strengthen the European component of NATO and for Europe to increase its relf-reliance. From this sprang the resolution to form a European Rapid Reaction Force. Forward basing and the pre-positioning of supplies being no longer practical on the same scale as before, the need arises to improve force mobility. The only way to provide a genuine rapid reaction force is by re-

equipping European forces with new transport fleets capable of transporting battle-winning equipment and troops and and keeping them supplied by air.

The design features of the FLA are: 1. Troops, heavy weapons and helicopters deployed by FLA direct from Europe to forward combat areas; 2. High cruising speed increases aircraft and aircrew utilisation and reduces aircrew and passenger fatigue; 3. Safe operation (three-engine take-off) from semi-prepared airstrips 3,000ft (915m) or less; 4. 90ft (28m) turning circle with autonomous back-up and minimum support for "go anywhere" capability; 5. Quiet cabin environment of high-bypass turbofan-powered FLA minimises aircrew and passenger fatigue; 6. Reduced mission cancellations and good survivability provided by safe, all-weather operations at low level and good system redundancy.

Compared with typical older generation tactical transports in current service FLA will offer: 1. 40 per cent savings in maintenance, manpower and aircrew; 60 per cent saving in ownership cost per payload tonne - n.m./hr. FLA transport quickly re-rôled into; 2. Point tanker, centreline hose and drogue 3-point tanker variant. Patrol capability of FLA long-range maritime patrol derivative, equal or superior to current maritime patrol aircraft. FLA

Above: **Carrying the famous name of Globemaster II the McDonnell Douglas C-17 is a long-range heavy lift cargo transport.** *(JM)*

Right: **The European FLA (Future Large Aircraft) will offer military Rapid Reaction Forces a major increase in their deployment capability. The FLA has twice the cargo volume and almost double the maximum payload compared to the stretched C-130J. The design of the FLA is at an advanced stage and is based firmly on the detailed needs of eight European air force.** *(BAe)*

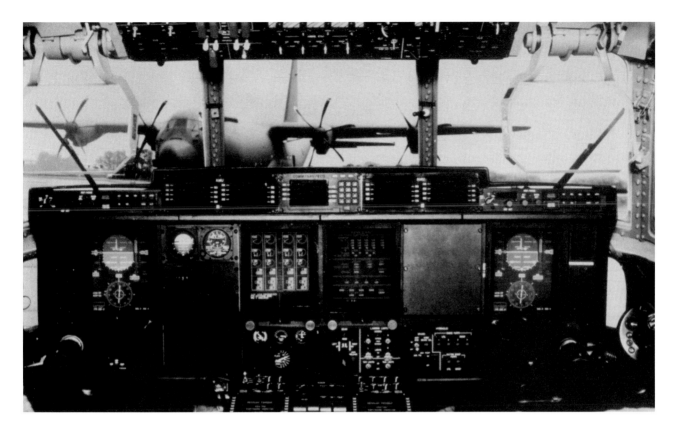

will utilise modern technology with systems and engine reliability proven in service (e.g. Airbus). FLA being designed as a low technical risk project.

The FLA is important for the future aerospace industry. New aircraft programmes are infrequent. A new military transport aircraft for Europe in the 100-short tonne short range class is essential for the European aerospace industry in order to ensure continuing development of design and technology as well as sales, both domestic and export. Europe does not merely need the use of a new aircraft, it needs to design and build it. European systems manufacturers are as good as any in the world, but individual companies lack the funds for research and development and the huge domestic market of those in the USA; collectively, they could match both. A European FLA needs and deserves the support of Government, the armed forces and industry.

Progress with the FLA programme has suffered from the usual difficulties that have handicapped every enterprise in which European states, with the disparities in technology and funds between the large and small nations, have collaborated. The requirement is obvious and has been formulated in the European Staff Requirement signed by eight countries. European industry has demonstrated its ability to finance the development phase. What is missing is a firm political commitment to the eventual procurement of the FLA as industry will develop it based on the European Staff Requirement and not merely to an undefined future large aircraft.

On 5 June 1995 it was decided to establish Airbus Military Company (AMC). On 5 June 1996 the French Government announced that no money would be available for development of the FLA. The French Minister of Defence conceded only the equivalent of a tentative US$125 million as an initial fund to purchase, early in the next century, whatever large military aircraft will be available. Also in June 1996, the German Government abnegated development funding for the FLA. Both countries had been regarded as its most enthusiastic supporters and biggest potential customers: between them, they were expected to buy 150 of the estimated Europe-wide 300.

Later in 1996 all eight companies made a proposal: they were willing to fund development for the first two years from their own resources, provided that their Governments would make a firm commitment to eventual purchase of the aircraft (number not specified) and make a substantial down payment. Industry has completed the tasks it was asked to and made sensible proposals. The best-informed opinions are that unless these are accepted and put into effect soon, the entire project will be cancelled and never revived. Instead, a USA or Russian/Ukranian design will replace it.

In December 1996 the United Kingdom decided half the RAF's needs would be sataisfied by buying 25 Lockheed C-130J and the balance could consist of the FLA, which, if it is ever built, will be bigger than the C-130J and capable of carrying Puma helicopters as well as multiple-launch rocket systems.

Above: **The cockpit of the latest Lockheed Hercules; C-130J. In the background is a mock-up of the aircraft.**
(Lockheed)

Index

Reference to photographs shown in *italics*

Lockheed C-130 Hercules. *(Lockheed)*